how to be a good parent

Family Matters

how to be
a good parent

Denise Robertson

Little Books by Big Names™

To my children and grandchildren,
with love

First published in the United Kingdom in 2003 by Little Books Ltd,
48 Catherine Place, London SW1E 6HL

10 9 8 7 6 5 4 3 2 1

Text copyright © 2003 by Denise Robertson
Design and layout copyright © 2003 by Little Books Ltd
Illustrations © by Gray Joliffe

A CIP catalogue record for this book is available from the British Library.

ISBN: 1 904435 01 7

The author and publisher will be grateful for any information that will
assist them in keeping future editions up-to-date. Although all reasonable care
has been taken in the preparation of this book, neither the publisher, editors nor
the author can accept any liability for any consequences arising from the use
thereof, or the information contained therein.

Many thanks to: Jamie Ambrose for editorial management, Eluned Jones
for proofreading, Gray Joliffe for illustrations, Ghost for jacket styling and
illustration, Mousemat Design for jacket and text design, Margaret Campbell
of Scan-Hi Digital and Craig Campbell of QSP Print for printing consultancy,
and Ann Barrett for indexing. Printed and bound in Scotland by Scotprint.

contents

A child is a gift for life,
the only miracle that improves with time.

introduction

There's no getting around it: having a baby changes your life. You become a mother or a father in addition to being an individual or a loving partner. Suddenly, you are responsible for another human being, and the prospect can be both wonderful and frightening.

For some women, the baby growing within them will be a personality almost from the moment of conception. They come to know its temperament, its likes and dislikes; they almost know its face. In the nine months they carry their son or daughter, he or she becomes a friend. For most mothers, however, the child they look down on seconds after it leaves their body is a mysterious stranger: an object of curiosity, awe, affection and enormous trepidation.

Nothing will ever be the same again once your baby is born, and there may be times when you will resent the demands your baby makes upon you and your adult lifestyle. Please: don't feel guilty about this. The mother or father who has never looked at a baby and thought, 'What have I *done*?' is either a saint – or has given birth to one. Most babies are impatient, and, until they get to know and trust you, even dictatorial. Yet they bring with them a special magic.

This book is designed to help you over the bad bits so that you do not miss a single moment of that magic. And on a technical note, in order not to litter the following pages with the artificial 'he or she', I have alternated masculine and feminine pronouns throughout. After all, babies, like parents, come in both genders.

Whether male or female, a child is a gift for life, the only miracle that improves with time. Whatever your circumstances, I hope this book will help you to enjoy every step of the journey.

Writing this book has made me broody, and has brought back those well-remembered sensations of touch and smell, sight and sound of children in the home.

Don't expect your child to conform exactly to textbook ideas of what a child should be. Trust your instincts, and above all, take pleasure in your children. Remember: each one of them is unique and therefore special. So are you, their parent. Enjoy each other.

1

how to be a
happy parent

The most important resource your baby has is *you*. That is why, as a parent, it is so important to make time for yourself. This is not being selfish; it's the very opposite, because you're doing it to protect your baby's future, and thus the future of your family as a whole. And making time for yourself begins long before your first baby is born.

Preparing for the birth

Both parents, but particularly new mothers, should resist the temptation to buy too much for the baby before the birth. Your midwife or maternity unit will give you a list of what items you will need. It will be minimal, but, if you have someone who will shop for you, wait until you see what presents are given by family and friends. Most gifts will be first-size outfits, and babies grow so quickly that it's a real pity to overbuy.

Some partners will enjoy preparing for a coming birth. Others, however, may show less enthusiasm. This is not a sign that they don't care; they may simply feel ill-equipped to advise or enthuse and so tend to shy away from the subject, but once their baby is in the world, they'll usually feel differently.

Once upon a time, men were shut out of labour wards. This was arbitrary and cruel to couples who wanted to share the moment of birth. Now the pendulum has swung to the other extreme and it is practically compulsory for fathers to be there. Discuss this prospect together and decide what you both want.

If you are to bring up your baby successfully, you will need to know when to follow your instincts; this is a good place to start. If you are each happy with the idea of a 'joint delivery', that's fine. If not, insist on your right to choose. For many couples, sharing that moment can be unbelievably rewarding. For a few, however, it isn't a joyful experience and they should resist pressure to conform.

After the birth

Once the first child is born, a mother may find that her relationship with her partner has changed. If the new father has had no experience with babies, his attitude may be disappointing, but his hesitation probably has much more to do with fear of such a tiny newcomer than with indifference.

As new parents, either one of you may resent the amount of attention that is given to the baby; when you feel like this, you feel guilty. Don't worry: these feelings are temporary and understandable. We're all human.

Once life in the house settles down and the baby is established in a routine, you'll have time to be man and woman again, but don't try to establish a routine too soon. Get to know your baby first.

Take care of yourself

Try to get as much sleep as you can. This means taking it when you can get it at first. It can help if you and your partner share night duty; if the off-duty partner can sleep in a separate room, that will make for sounder sleep. These emergency measures won't be needed for more than a few weeks, so don't worry that the loving companionship of the double bed is gone forever.

The enormous fatigue you may feel in the initial weeks won't last. At first, feeding on demand allows little or no planning, but soon you'll be moving towards feeding at three-hour intervals – and getting your lives back on track.

Make time to be together

If you're part of a loving relationship, you need to have time together as man and woman without one ear cocked for that little whimper. If you're on your own, it's even more important to recharge your batteries. Push yourself too far, and your baby will suffer, so nourish yourself as carefully as you nourish your child.

Build in time for play and laughter, just as you build in those times for your son or daughter. Deal with worries so that you, too, have a healthy, safe environment. Above all, do these things without guilt, because you do them in order to secure your child's future.

Of course, this is counsel of perfection. There may not be money for a quiet meal out or a grandma to babysit so that you can take a walk in the countryside. Yet you must do what you can.

If money is tight, put a little aside until your treat can be afforded. If babysitting is a problem, contact one of the organizations listed on pages 184–7 and try to sort out mutual, occasional child care.

And remember: no one says sex belongs only to bedtime. Occasional lovemaking in some precious stolen moment can keep your relationship alive. If you can arrange these liaisons at a time when your child is safe elsewhere, all the better.

No one would deny that you derive enormous joy from being with your child, but as parents, you still need refreshment. And think of the sweetness of coming back to find your baby waiting after a well-deserved break! It's worth the separation.

DIFFERENT TYPES OF PARENTS

Sometimes a child will come into your life through adoption or step-parenthood, or you may be facing parenthood alone. The magic can be the same, but coping must, of necessity, be different. Today's families come in all shapes and sizes, so although this book is for parents in any situation, some families face additional issues.

Adoption

Those parents who have thought carefully about adoption will be prepared for the event of a child coming into their home. The adoption process is lengthy, complicated and often frustrating, but those who make it to the end of the vetting process can be sure they're not acting on impulse. Equally, their children can be sure that they were really wanted.

It's important to be truthful about your child's origins, and the sooner this becomes an established fact, the better. 'We chose you and you are special' is a good message to impart. Be prepared for questions, and if you can, make it clear that you will not find those questions hurtful. A child will naturally have curiosity about its birth parents, but may wonder whether such questions will seem disloyal to the adoptive parents it loves.

Remember that the parent who nurtures is the important parent. Your child will learn from your example and return any affection it receives. When conflict arises, see it for what it is: the natural friction between child and parent that is part of child development.

If you have adopted an older child, don't expect immediate mutual affection. You need to grow together. As you show respect and concern, the child will relax and feel secure – but this process takes time.

Most children eligible for adoption have been let down in the past. Naturally, they will be cautious about giving their trust. but that doesn't mean they never will. Indeed, the very things that make them cautious will eventually make them appreciative.

Don't feel that you have to be 'superparent'. Your new child may have talents and abilities you don't share. As long as you give him the opportunity to achieve his potential, you don't have to drive yourself to play piano or excel at sports. Glory in your differences; your role is to encourage, not to compete.

It can help to draw a family tree showing your child firmly in place. Explain his position in the family and be prepared to talk about that other unknown family. The older child may hint that he needs to know more. Many organizations can help with these problems (see pages 184–7).

A child given in adoption is both a gift and a responsibility – which makes it exactly like a child born to you in the usual way. If things go wrong or conflict arises, never assume it is because an adopted child isn't 'yours'. Conflict is natural at times, and in my experience, occurs just as often (if not more so) in the birth situation as it does after adoption.

Step-parenting

No parent or step-parent should expect a child to welcome coming together as a new family with open arms. If a divorced birth parent is involved, children may feel disloyal in welcoming a substitute. If the step-parent appears too soon after bereavement, a child may not have had time to adjust. If too long a gap ensues, a child may look upon the surviving parent as his personal property and resent the incoming adult. Younger children find it easier to adjust to a step-parent than an older child, and it's possible that an estranged parent may add to any division.

Now that I've listed all the drawbacks, let me confirm that it *is* possible to have a good step-relationship. Let it grow gradually. Too many step-parents 'start as they mean to go on' because they feel unsure of their position. I hear stories of new stepmothers who ban stepchildren from areas of the home where previously they were free to go, or of stepfathers who see their role as disciplinarian because a mother on her own has allowed rules to relax. This is counter-productive. Respect those rights the child had before you came; where it makes sense to take them over, do it gradually. Allow child and birth parent to spend time alone together and respect the child's privacy. Eventually, if he doesn't feel threatened, he will concede rights to you.

When combining two sets of children, scrupulous fairness is essential. If there are conflicting family rules – for instance, over bedtimes – discuss how a compromise can be reached. Most children will see the sense of cooperation, but it may take time.

If a new baby comes on the scene, it can act as a binding force, but the existing children of both marriages will need reassurance that they have equal status with the newcomer.

The stereotypical picture of a step-parent is of a wicked witch or a bullying tyrant. In fact, step-parents can play a vital role in a child's life and become not only a parent but a friend.

If you need help with the step-situation, contact some of the helplines on pages 184–7.

Single parents

Single parenthood can arise through broken relationships or death. Most often, the single parent is a mother, but the number of single fathers is increasing. Most single parents have to work to support their child, and it can be hard to assume the role of sole parent as well at the end of a working day. Sometimes, there is friction with the absent parent, or, if there is no other parent living or interested in the child, there are almost constant decisions to take without support or discussion.

The lone parent may be led into the trap of seeing his or her child as another adult: someone with whom to discuss the pros and cons of decisions or to confide in. Although this is understandable, it's not always wise. Frequent consultation can make it difficult to establish authority when you need to, and it can lead to a child feeling weighed down with responsibility. This kind of camaraderie increases the bond between parent and child, but it also increases dependence on each other. The child may become too concerned over her parent's emotional welfare to voice her own fears, or, if money is in short supply, to talk about needs at school or play.

It can also create trauma if a new partner appears on the scene. Access to the other parent can help avoid this situation, and grandparents, too, can play a useful role. Support is also available from self-help organizations (see pages 184–7).

Obviously, it is in the child's interest that arrangements are amicable. Where hostility exists between separated parents, a child should not be drawn in. Yet children are perceptive. If you can't avoid their exposure to tension, tell them that the relationship is not easy, but because both parents share love for them, they will always work together. Cooperating also means that the custodial parent can get some much-needed time off.

A lone parent needs to make extra time to listen, and this isn't easy when you're juggling work and home lives. Also, you need to allow your children to talk about their other parent without making them feel disloyal. It isn't easy, but it will make your relationship with your children a healthier one.

Listening with interest to the doings of a partner who may have betrayed you demands that you be a saint for a while; this makes it all the more important to have a place *you* can get emotional support. If there are no available friends or family members, get in touch with Gingerbread or one of the organizations listed on pages 184–7.

A lone parent should appoint a guardian to care for any children in the event of his or her death. If both parents are alive but separated, they can share parental responsibility. This means that each of them has responsibility while the children are in their care, but it does not mean they can take life-changing decisions without consulting the other parent.

Absent parents

Sometimes an absent parent must be barred from access for good reasons. Sometimes absent parents choose to be indifferent. In some cases, a loving parent has died and ceased to be a presence in your child's life. In all three instances, a child may still be curious about that other half of the equation. Photographs can help, so can recalling happy memories. If you can, paint a picture of the past that is acceptable but not untruthful.

Lying to save a child pain seldom works. Mothers who present gifts they have bought as being 'from your father' are creating an illusion that cannot be sustained. It's better to be truthful, but there is no need to say 'Your father forgot your birthday because he doesn't give a damn.' That's taking truth a step too far.

While single parenthood can sometimes be an uphill struggle, the rewards are many, and the child of single parents can fare just as well in later life as the child from a two-parent family.

Having been a single parent, I know the strain of being 'on duty' twenty-four hours a day. Yet once your child becomes a happy adult, you'll realize all that effort has been more than worthwhile.

Working mothers

Leaving your child for the first time can be very painful. Try not to feel guilty. Helping your child to make relationships with others is vital. As long as you have done your best to provide good care, see the separation as an important part of your child's development.

However, if leaving a young baby makes you unbelievably unhappy, do everything you can to go back to work later or work part-time. Often, women have to juggle a desire to stay with the baby and maintain their standard of living. This must be an individual decision, but weigh things carefully before you decide.

The arguments for and against working mothers have always raged, and will continue to do so, often causing great distress. My own view is that the quality of a child's life is not damaged by its mother working, as long as its welfare remains the paramount concern. If you are undecided, then consider the following questions.

- Must you work to maintain a reasonable standard of living?
- Is the child care you have put in place more than adequate?
- Would remaining at home all day make you miserable and unfulfilled?

If you answer 'Yes' to all three, then you should go ahead without guilt. If you answer 'No' to any of them, you need more discussion. Remember that this is a central question for *both* parents to consider – and grandparents, too, if they are to be involved in child care.

2

how to have a
happy baby

In the first few days of parenthood you may wonder quite what you've let yourself in for. Deprived of sleep, obsessed with 'getting things right', there may be moments when you feel like running away. Again, don't feel guilty about such feelings, but do rest assured: you won't always feel like this.

Bonding

You will have heard the word 'bonding' being bandied about, I'm sure. It means the instant rapport that is supposed to occur the moment a mother sets eyes on her child. For some mothers, this is exactly what happens. For others, it takes longer, so don't worry if, for some medical reason, you don't see your child immediately or you don't get that 'instant' feeling when you do.

A baby is pre-programmed to bond, and once you have the opportunity to hold her, to feed and get to know her, bonding will come. In fact, it is a while before she will be able to differentiate between adults and know who is her mother, so you have plenty of time to establish closeness. What is important for emotional well-being and future adult relationships is that, in the first few years of life, a child does form a close relationship with at least one adult.

Don't worry that an inability to breast-feed will hinder bonding. It's the closeness and the holding during the feeding process that strengthens the link between mother and baby – and father and baby, too. The father who bottle-feeds his baby is also forging valuable links.

Beating the 'baby blues'

It's extremely important for new mothers to share the early days with a partner or willing grandparents or friends. You will feel a little weary and perhaps overwhelmed; you may feel weepy or extra-sensitive. Don't worry. This is a natural process as your body adjusts to the end of pregnancy. Sometimes known as the 'baby blues', it usually begins about the third day and it doesn't last.

Post-natal depression, a more severe form of the baby blues, occurs in about fifteen percent of mothers, but for many of them, it is short-lived. For a few, it can lead to feelings of inadequacy, insomnia, loss of appetite and a disinclination to bond with and care for the baby. The important thing to grasp is that this is a *physical* condition, probably of hormonal origin; in no way does it represent a failing as a mother. The condition responds to treatment with anti-depressants and therapy, and eventually your love-affair with your baby will be back on track.

In these early days, don't fret about housework. Attend to the essentials: caring for your baby and making sure everyone, including you, eats. And try to have a visitor policy. People will want to see the new baby, but stagger visits and don't feel you have to leap around making everyone happy.

Lack of sleep is the constant complaint of

all new parents. Take turns to sleep when you can, whatever the time of day, but try to remember this stage won't last forever. When you do get a chance to sleep because someone else is in charge, do so right away so that you don't lie there with one ear cocked for trouble.

Eventually, you'll develop a routine that will bring ease to you and give your growing child a feeling of security because she knows there are certain landmarks through the day and week. Yet routine should never be so rigid that it rules your life. Certainly in these early days it should not even be considered.

Time management

Make life easier by keeping all you need for nappy changing in a bag that goes where the baby goes. That means you don't have to run up and down stairs looking for baby supplies. The easier you make things, the more time you'll have to enjoy watching your baby. Don't forget to take photographs; so many changes take place during the first few weeks of life, that you'll want to look back on them later.

On the subject of nappies, always keep a wad of cotton wool handy if you're changing a baby boy. In the early days, a baby boy is apt to pee as soon as his penis is uncovered – and his range is impressive! Always wipe your baby girl from front to back, to prevent bacteria from her anus getting near her vagina.

And don't worry about the colour of early motions. If you're breast-feeding, what you've eaten can influence the shade. Always consult your doctor or health visitor if you're really worried, but remember there is no absolute norm.

The crying game

It is natural for your newborn to cry. It is his only means of communication. Research suggests that babies cry for about two hours a day during the first few weeks, which then tapers off as you learn to anticipate your baby's needs.

When crying starts, check to see if your baby needs changing or feeding, is too hot or cold, or is in an uncomfortable position. A baby with tummy pain will draw up his knees and the cry will be more piercing. Talk in a reassuring way or pick the baby up for a cuddle. Walking with him in your arms or pushing him in a pram helps.

Don't make the mistake of thinking he is crying because you have let him down in some way. Crying is natural, so keep your cool. Eventually it will cease, the baby will sleep and you can have a nice cup of tea.

If you feel at the end of your tether, make the baby comfortable, then go into another room for a while. If the crying persists for too long, or you feel that you just can't cope, contact one of the helplines on pages 184–7. You'll find someone on the other end of the line who will understand.

TWINS

If you've been gifted with twins, each baby should develop as normal, but you will have to adjust feeding, bathing, etc, to accommodate two little bodies. Twins also make special demands on parents when it comes to loss of sleep. Fortunately, in the UK, at least one organization can advise on multiple births (page 189). Meanwhile, here are some helpful tips.

It is important to treat twins as two children who just happen to have the same birthday. Even identical twins have differing thought processes and personalities, so while it's tempting to see them as two halves of a whole, this can be a mistake.

Feeding

In the beginning, the prospect of two needy babies can be daunting. It's good to feed them individually whenever you can, but if that's not always possible, two big squares of sorbo rubber with a baby-shaped scoop out of each can be positioned on either side of you to help hold a baby comfortably to each breast. Later, dad or a trusted adult can feed one while you attend to the other. Don't drive yourself wild with worry over whether or not baby A has had ten minutes more of your time than baby B, but do try to apportion your love equally.

Bathing

At bathtime, avoid having both babies in the water at once unless there is another adult on hand. In the time it takes to lift one child out and carry it to another room, its sibling could drown. If you're on your own, bring a high-chair into the bathroom and let one baby watch in safety while the other is in the water. Baby shops are geared to deal with multiple-birth requirements and you'll soon adjust to the practical demands of twins.

Friends

There is no doubt that there is a bond between children who have shared a womb, but they should be encouraged to explore their differing potentials and have separate circles of friends. Too often, parents assume twins will be enough for each other and make less effort to encourage friendships outside the home. Later, in their school lives, twins may need to go separate ways; if they are used to socializing independently from an early age, this will be easier.

Rearing two individuals

It may be necessary to have a shared wardrobe at first, but, where possible, let each twin develop individual tastes in dress. Spend time alone with each child when you can, and make sure that both get to make choices. And try not to refer to them as 'the twins'. Loving parents will say 'Peter and John and the twins' when, they should say 'Peter and John and Mary and Margaret.'

Often one twin will be more vocal and outgoing than another and will almost dictate events for both of them. This is a natural process and not a fault in the dominant one, but if parents aren't careful, the less outgoing twin can become almost a shadow of her stronger sibling.

While rearing twins presents a special set of problems, the pleasure of seeing two children with a shared bond more than makes up for the extra work.

DEVELOPMENT

Every child is different; thus, development differs in every case. However, the following is a rough guide to the progress your baby will make as he grows towards school age.

At birth

Your baby is conscious of changes in temperature, bright lights, being handled, and the comfort and closeness of another human body. He has no control over his own body because his nervous system is not yet sufficiently developed. His head is disproportionate to his body; his legs are small and weak, and all he can do for himself is breathe, suck, turn his head a little and cry. Can you blame him for exercising his lungs vigorously from time to time?

A new baby may put his fingers to his mouth and likes being upright because he can see more clearly than when he is lying down. He is startled by sudden noises and doesn't like the sensation of falling, so always lower him gently into a cot or pram. But very soon after the birth he begins to recognize the nipple or the teat and will show excitement when put to the breast. He sleeps about sixteen to eighteen hours and feeds about ten times a day.

One month

By this time, your baby has settled into a routine. She has discovered that she can exercise her hands and enjoys spreading her fingers, sucking a thumb or even a fist. Her arms will stretch out occasionally and sometimes the fingers of one hand will explore the other. Similarly, free from nappy and clothing, the legs will move, and the toes will spread and wiggle.

Your baby may begin to lift its head for a second, especially when held against your shoulder. Her eyes will follow objects moving close to her face and she will be soothed by the human voice – except when she's hungry and refuses to be pacified. Above all, the month-old baby will appreciate security, warmth and the sensation of being loved. She can meet your gaze and smile. She knows her mother by smell and sound.

Three months

A personality is emerging now. Your baby is alert and enjoys company. He will smile and make noises other than crying and will try to roll onto his side. He kicks with his legs and enjoys pushing with his feet against the foot of the pram or cot or his mother's hands. He enjoys being walked in mother's or father's arms and wants to be part of the company, but will lie contentedly in his cot after feeding, kicking and gurgling.

Remember, all babies are different. If your baby hates to lie down or be left for a second, don't despair; all phases pass with time. And if your baby was smaller than usual at birth, don't worry. There will be a gradual catching-up process. By school age, you should see little or no difference.

Six months

Your baby will have doubled her birth weight and grown about five inches. She can wriggle about on her stomach or sit up in her pram, propped on a cushion. She can handle toys now and loves to wave them about. She practices sounds and will enjoy your 'oohs' and 'aahs' of approval. She will try to support herself on her legs and pull herself up on furniture; she also chews everything she can find because her teeth are almost ready to emerge.

She likes to have toys offered to her and will offer them back, but is not yet able to open her grasp and let go. She loves to be bounced on someone's knee or in her cot and enjoys being sung to or engaged in conversation. However, she can now recognize all 'her' people: family, siblings or friends. Because of this, she will probably not immediately smile at strangers, and will only respond when she feels certain that they are friendly.

Nine months

This is the time to move your ornaments to a higher shelf. Your baby is mobile now, can crawl from place to place, and will be attracted to things like trailing flexes or objects he can handle and put in his mouth.

Make sure your home is child-safe so that you can relax and watch your baby explore. It may take time to child-proof every room, but it's easier than frustrating your baby by jumping up every few minutes to take something from him. He will enjoy family times, especially the more boisterous ones, kicking and moving his body to show delight. Bathtimes are especially pleasurable, and simple scoops and cartons will give endless enjoyment.

By now he will probably be having three

meals a day. He can hold his own mug with two hands and will try to grab and wield the spoon. If his mother doesn't allow him the use of the spoon, he may respond with a temper tantrum and a stiffening of his whole body. The answer is to provide a second spoon, and just make sure a sufficient amount of food gets eaten. He 'feeds' himself and doesn't at all mind that most of it ends up on his bib.

Twelve months

At a year old, your baby can pull himself up on the furniture and then move sideways. He can let go and stand for a minute or may even stagger forward if you hold his hand. He can use his thumb and forefinger as pincers and can now let go of things at will. This means he can throw things out of the pram or cot – and this usually becomes a favourite game.

He chatters away much of the time, using words like 'Ma-ma' or 'Dad-dad', and will now play alone quite happily – although he likes to know mum or dad are near. He is more accepting of strangers, especially if they are willing to play 'peek-a-boo', and understands simple words such as 'bath' and 'walk', even if he cannot repeat them.

Up to two years

Your child will concentrate on improving her mobility, negotiating stairs, walking, balancing, climbing chairs and moving her toys, especially if they have wheels. Once she has mastered movement, she will concentrate on speech. She wants the undivided attention of mother or carer and will resort to crying if ignored.

Independence usually assumes enormous importance at this stage. She wants to feed herself and will only allow herself to be dressed if the process is quick; there is so much to do and explore that fastening buttons and straps seems a colossal waste of time. She is fascinated by fitting things together and putting one object inside another. Toys get rough treatment now, especially if they don't do what is wanted.

Although control of bowel and bladder is still far off, it helps to introduce a potty which can be used on the odd occasion that mum sees something coming in time.

Words come easily now. By her second birthday, your daughter's vocabulary will encompass up to 200 words.

Up to three years

Although a child's third year is physically demanding, for a parent, the rewards are huge. Your child has become full of energy. He is heavy to lift because he weighs up to two stone and stands thirty to thirty-two inches high. He runs easily, climbs energetically and loves to copy everything mum or dad does. His favourite word may well be 'No' and temper tantrums may come fairly often, but he can be diverted and loves to think he is cooperating.

This is also a time when nightmares may occur or fear of the dark begins. Don't be alarmed by these fears; they are symptoms of his developing imagination, and with comfort and reassurance, they will pass.

Be tolerant, too, of what may appear to be temper tantrums. He has learned to be angry, but doesn't yet know how to control his anger. He is worried by unusual occurrences (such as mum not being where he expected her to be) and he is horrified by what seems like anger or distress in a loved one. And he does not yet know that what occurs in dreams is imaginary.

Don't imagine the third year is all gloom. The comedian in your child begins to emerge. He enjoys dressing up, making you laugh, playing word or finger games and, as his third birthday approaches, 'helping' in family rituals like tidying up or table laying. He will probably have daytime control of bladder and bowels and be proud of using his potty. By two-and-a-half or so, he will have a full set of milk teeth.

Up to four years

Most babyhood problems will have gone by now. There may still be night-time bedwetting or the occasional daytime accident, but these are best treated lightly. Your daughter will run and jump, ride a tricycle and climb with confidence. She can use pencil and crayons and cut with child-proof scissors, but more precise finger movements will still be difficult.

Her favourite words will be 'what', 'where' and 'how', and there will be a new word every day. The companionship of other children becomes all-important now, and the important lessons of sharing and taking turns comes into play.

In the absence of other children, toys become 'people'. Dolls are bathed and dressed or treated for 'poorly tummies', and rows of toy figures become armies to be advanced upon. At nursery or playgroup, the three-year-old also learns that adults outside the family can be trusted.

Up to five years

The four-year-old child is keen on independence but will respond to reason. Holding hands to cross a busy road or in crowds makes sense as long as he is not so constrained when safety is reached. He knows when adults behave unfairly and likes an apology. He can control his emotions and will show a great deal of patience when building a model or playing with Lego™. He may have a 'special friend' now, but will turn to a parent or teacher for help when needed.

Now is the time to show him how to find answers for himself. Even small children can use picture encyclopedias or computers, but if the answer cannot be found there, an adult who will help is essential.

Sometimes the personality of four-year-olds may seem to change. They may become bossy or aggressive, enjoy disobeying or being rude or silly. This can simply be independence taken too far, or it may be boredom. Be tolerant: use diversions and concentrate on showing your child respect. Giving the rebel a task to carry out, such as feeding the rabbit, will produce a better result than a lecture or a threat of retribution.

Watch out, too, for signs of apprehension of school. Some children look forward to school as a huge adventure. For others, it can seem like prison and they need reassurance.

LANGUAGE

I was once reprimanded by an aunt for using 'baby talk' to my infant son, 'He won't be able to speak properly when he grows up,' she said. She was wrong. Before long, I was wondering how to stop an extremely articulate toddler from talking non-stop.

Talk to your child from the moment of birth in the way that seems most natural to you. Some mothers croon a language of their own; others recite their favourite nursery rhymes. The words don't matter. The baby knows it is being addressed, and that is the important issue.

Your voice should bring an almost immediate response from your baby. Failure to react by turning towards you or gurgling in return could indicate a hearing loss. If this happens, don't panic (even small babies may daydream), but if it happens repeatedly or loud noises fail to startle, mention it to your health visitor. Use your voice to soothe your baby when it is fretful and, as the baby develops, show pleasure at the sounds it makes for you.

The beginnings of conversation

At around two months, your baby will show a desire to communicate verbally. Encourage this. You'll be amazed at how much they convey by gurgling.

Some experts believe children have an innate ability to learn a language, but there's no doubt that children who grow up in a verbally rich environment learn faster. Your baby will start to imitate your sounds. A particular favourite may be 'B' or 'M'. Have fun with sounds.

You'll probably find you're using 'Motherese' – a way of speaking slowly and distinctly with spaces between the words: 'Where... is... my... lovely... baby... boy?' Motherese has a rhythm to it, which a baby likes, and it contains a lot of repetition, which is comforting.

Most experts disapprove of using 'baby language' words like 'moo-moo' and 'bow-wow'. It's better to use proper words such as 'cow' and 'dog', but if 'bow-wow' and 'gee-gee' come naturally to your lips, don't be afraid of them or worry that you're doing harm. The most important thing of all is that you and your baby should enjoy conversing. Don't forget to listen attentively even when the sounds don't make sense. Without that encouragement, why should your baby bother to learn to speak?

As the baby becomes a toddler, talk through everyday routines. 'Here is your lunch.' 'Good: you seem to like that.' 'Shall we put on your new dress?' Simple phrases like these, especially when you hold up the object, are helping your child begin the ascent of language, a mountain of words, some of which contain more than one meaning. The sooner you start, the better.

And don't forget action rhymes such as 'Round and round the garden'. The look of pleasure on the face of the smallest child as it waits for the familiar punchline of a gentle tickle is a glorious sight. Enjoy picture books together, pointing out objects and naming them or, better still, waiting for your child to name them. To a child, reading the same story again and again is reassuring, so stifle your yawns and content yourself with introducing new books from time to time.

Developing listening skills

It's important to encourage your child to listen. Even at an early stage you can help develop the ability to obey requests and absorb information, abilities that will be invaluable later on in nursery and school.

When you say, 'Please come here,' make sure your child does come, putting out a welcoming hand if necessary. Remember that even a very young child likes to understand the reason for such requests. Saying 'Please come here because…' produces a better reaction than 'Because I say so.'

At about three years of age, a child's language increases in both volume and complexity. We've all heard the harassed mother in the supermarket begging her child not to ask one more blankety-blank question! Understanding how your child sees the world around it will help you find the necessary patience to answer those questions in a straightforward way. Don't be afraid to say 'I don't know,' but recognize that this is only a temporary answer. Say, instead, 'I don't know, but when we get home, we'll find out.'

Psychologists believe that the use of a child's name helps him to absorb new information, so when you ask Daddy or Gran if they know the answer, personalize the question if you can. 'Paula wants to know why her ball is round,' is more relevant to your child than, 'Why is a ball round?'

Sometimes questions can be difficult,

especially when they concern vital matters such as sex and death. I think truth is important, but that doesn't mean you have to explain the fine details of the *Kama Sutra* to the three-year-old who simply asks 'Where do babies come from?'

Above all, remember that language, as with everything else, develops at different rates in different children. Some will string words together fluently at eighteen months. Others may reach that stage at three.

Girls tend to develop their language skills sooner than boys, but early talkers are not necessarily more intelligent than late talkers. However, if your two-year-old child isn't forming some words, it may indicate hearing difficulties and should be investigated.

Physical activity

New parents may long for their tiny baby to move. The first time that small head raises itself from the pillow, the first time he pulls himself erect, the first wobbly step… these are moments parents treasure. But from the first triumphant moment that your baby realizes he can manage to turn over, he can never again be left unattended on a high surface.

A safe environment

On a blanket on the floor, far away from sharp corners or objects that might be pulled over, your child can gradually become mobile. This happens at around nine months to a year. You can offer encouragement by placing a favourite toy just out of reach or by holding out your arms from a distance.

Some children crawl, others 'bottom shuffle' or 'walk' from one vantage point to another. The moment when they at last stand alone is thrilling for a child. He will crow with delight before toppling over because he knows a milestone has been reached.

The instant a child becomes mobile, his parents should prepare to say goodbye to an easy life. Toddlers can move with the speed of light and hate to be frustrated. Try to create 'safety zones': places where there are no breakable objects, where floors are cushioned by carpets and nothing can be pulled over; then you can sit and relax while your child explores. Resist the temptation to fasten a child in a high-chair or playpen too often. It may make you feel safe, but it makes your child feel imprisoned.

Coping with the ups and downs

When your child falls over – and this will happen quite often – be on hand to comfort but don't remark on the mishap. 'Oh dear, you're always falling over,' however lovingly said, can make a child feel clumsy and eventually expect to stumble. Saying, 'You're so good at walking,' has the opposite effect.

Be prepared for your child to fall in love with stairs; they hold a fascination for toddlers. At eighteen months, your child will probably go up on hands and knees or haul himself up the banister. Coming down is a bottom shuffle.

At two, he will take one step at a time, bringing the second foot up before attempting another step. At four, he can mount stairs like a grown-up, but will probably come down one step at a time. From then on progress is rapid. A five-year-old can hop, skip, run up and down stairs and climb anything in sight.

When to hold back

A parent's role is to encourage, keeping one eye on safety and the other on a child's self-esteem. I know the heart-stopping feeling that your precious baby is about to break his neck, but a child who is not allowed to use his body to the full is a frustrated and, eventually, unhappy one.

Physical activity creates other advantages. Active children breathe more deeply, absorbing more oxygen. Digestion is helped and waste products are more efficiently eliminated. Children who get plenty of exercise sleep better, and coordination of eye, brain and muscles is improved. Don't worry that a child will get over-tired. Unless he is spurred on, the average child will alternate activity with periods of rest, throwing himself down to daydream or listen to a story. Ten minutes later he'll be leaping around again, refreshed. It's important, too, to help children learn the exercise habit for later life.

Above all, try to remember that your child is unique and has his own schedule of development. Just because the child next door can catch or kick a ball at three and your child can't doesn't mean your child is backward. In all probability, your child is advanced in something else, or is simply developing at a more leisurely pace. If real worries persist, consult your doctor.

FEEDING YOUR BABY

It's universally acknowledged that 'breast is best', providing perfect nutrition and some immunity against disease, so breast-feed your baby if you possibly can. However, some mothers are not able to breast-feed, while others choose not to do so. It's important to make this decision for yourself and not be persuaded to breast-feed or bottle-feed against your will.

Talk to your midwife, and if you possibly can, give breast-feeding a try. You can switch to a bottle later if you choose, and both methods, properly applied, are good for your baby. In my opinion, the idea that breast-feeding makes for a closer bond is untrue. It's the holding and satisfying that forge the link.

Learning to breast-feed

Don't assume that breast-feeding is a simple matter of placing baby to nipple. At the beginning, it can be hard work as both you and baby get the hang of it. Your midwife will help, so don't be afraid to ask questions. Initially, your breasts may be uncomfortable, and as your baby realizes what a good thing he's onto, he may suck so vigorously that he gets a 'sucking blister' on his lip. Don't worry; these conditions soon disappear and feeding becomes a source of pleasure for both mother and baby. If you develop sore nipples, ask your midwife or doctor for help.

Positioning the baby correctly eases pressure on the nipple and you'll soon get the position right. Alternatively, you can express milk and feed the baby later. Ask your midwife to show you how to do this and store the milk safely in the refrigerator.

Bottle feeding

Always make up bottle feeds according to the instructions, and don't be tempted to pop in an extra scoop or make the feed weaker.

Keep the teat full of milk so that your baby doesn't suck in air, and burp him carefully several times during each feed, just as you do when breast-feeding. Hold your baby upright and gently rub or pat his back till you get a burp. It's worth doing this thoroughly because wind can cause tummy pain and disturbed sleep.

And enjoy feeding times, whether bottle or breast, as moments of tranquillity before weaning begins. At first, you should feed on demand, but as the weeks go by this settles into three feeds a day.

Breast- and bottle-fed babies are getting a balanced diet, and children over a year old should generally get whole milk in preference to skimmed or semi-skimmed. That can be given after the fifth birthday.

What foods does your child need?

Most experts believe that children who are offered a wide range of nutritious foods will eat healthily over a period of weeks. They may eat only orange segments for lunch on Monday or cheese on Tuesday, but in the long run, they'll eat a balanced diet. Many mothers are too afraid of malnutrition to allow their children this freedom. Instead, they watch each bite that enters their offspring's mouths and are racked with anxiety over mealtimes. To avoid such worries and ensure your growing child has all he or she needs, bear the following in mind.

Children need protein more than adults because their basic body tissue is growing quickly. Animal protein comes from eggs and dairy produce, meat and fish. Vegetable protein is derived from cereals, nuts, root vegetables and pulses. Carbohydrates, which produce energy, are present in sugary foods and starchy foods such as bread and potatoes. Some carbohydrate is essential, but when eaten to excess, it turns into body fat. The same is true of fat, which is found in meat, fish oil, butter and margarine, and some vegetables.

Fibre, which is sometimes called roughage, encourages digestion and discourages constipation. It is found in fruit and vegetables, wholemeal bread, wholegrain cereals, nuts and pulses. Check the content of breakfast cereals carefully to make sure that the beneficial effects of the fibre they contain are not outweighed by the salt and sugar content.

Vitamins and minerals are essential. Children need vitamin A, which is found in cheese, fish, eggs, chicken, spinach and carrots. Vitamin B comes from milk, liver, cheese and wholemeal bread. Vitamin C comes from fresh fruit and vegetables, especially citrus fruits. Vitamin D is found in fish oil, liver, dairy produce and sunshine, while Vitamin E is found in oats, brown rice, liver, wholegrain cereals and nuts.

Minerals such as calcium are found in milk, cheese, yoghurt and green vegetables. Iron comes from red meat, eggs, bread and green vegetables. Don't be alarmed by such a long list of requirements; a child's needs are small, and many foods provide most or several things at once.

Weaning

Weaning is necessary to provide a wider diet and to help develop the skills of biting and chewing. It's also an important step on the road to shared family meals.

At first, usually between four and six months, the aim of weaning is to accustom your baby to different tastes and textures. Breast or formula milk is still providing an ample diet, so don't worry if most of the solid food finds its way anywhere but in your baby's mouth. Baby cereals and fruit and vegetable purées are fine, although wheat-based cereals containing gluten could cause an allergic reaction at this stage.

Remember that your baby loves to be breast- or bottle-fed, safe in your arms. At first, she may reject spoon-feeding as different and 'unloving'. When you begin to wean, hold the baby in your arms, and give a small breast or bottle feed first. Use a plastic spoon or even a clean fingertip and be content to introduce a minute amount of food into the baby's mouth. Let her savour the new taste. Smile and make encouraging noises and don't get agitated if your baby rejects this new and strange substance. Finish with another small breast or bottle feed and try again next time.

Some mothers prefer to use proprietary brands. Others make their own fresh purées each time, but it's safe to make larger quantities and freeze in small portions as long as it is done carefully. At this stage, breast or bottle milk is still the most important part of the diet.

Between six and nine months, your baby will graduate to mashed or minced food, and wheat-based cereals can be included. Bread is acceptable, and finger foods such as pieces of fruit or carrot usually go down well because the baby sees this as independence. Homemade food is good because you can provide as much as the baby needs. Proprietary brands are limited on size, and may not be enough as your baby grows.

Foods that might cause choking, such as peanuts, popcorn, chunks of meat and hard vegetables, should be avoided. Yet however 'mushy' the food is, a tiny child should never eat without supervision.

Between nine and twelve months, babies learn to cope with most family foods although lumps still need to be mashed. Your baby will still need breast or formula milk in between the three meals a day, but bottles should be dispensed with generally by the first birthday. Your baby may miss the bottle, and if this is so, a dummy or soother can be substituted, but avoid dipping it in sweet stuff.

Although some salt is essential to tissue fluids, it's best to use it sparingly. Never add salt to a baby's food, and discourage toddlers from eating salty things such as crisps.

Vegetarians must always make sure that they feed their babies a wide variety of foods in sufficient quantity to supply their needs. Specialist advice on this is advisable.

Moving on to mealtimes

Once the process of weaning is complete, mealtimes should be enjoyable – not occasions for anxiety. Don't be alarmed if your child refuses a meal, and don't serve the refused food again; it doesn't become more palatable with time.

Also, don't heap plates with food. Huge amounts of food make a child feel pressured. With a small child, presenting simple finger food is often the answer for happy eating. Mealtimes should be happy occasions, the opportunity to talk and relax as much for children as adults.

Ideally, a child should not skip any meals, especially breakfast. After a night's sleep, energy levels are low, and a breakfast of cereals with fruit and milk, an egg with toast and a drink of the child's choice will top up the levels.

Every child will be faddy occasionally over

certain foods. If this is ignored, it will usually pass, but if a parent becomes obsessed with the need to include, say, sprouts or fish in the diet, a child may become almost proud of hating fish and glow when you tell family and friends of the struggle to get him to eat it. Try to rise above the conflict. Substitute a food with the same nutritional value and move on.

If your child is always food-resistant, don't let mealtimes become a battleground. Keep meals simple. Slogging for hours to produce new *cordon bleu* dishes won't necessarily produce an appetite. Make food attractive and don't worry too much about table manners. Finger-eating is better than no eating. When you think there'll be no more progress, lift the toddler from his high- chair or let the older child leave the table. There's nothing to be gained by keeping a sullen or weepy child in place; he will only associate future meals with conflict.

Whether or not there is a problem, discuss menus with your child. Ask which vegetable would look nice with which type of meat or fish, and allow the odd eccentricity. Combinations that make you gag may well appeal to your child. Allowing choice makes young children feel in control and well-disposed towards food, especially if they can be involved in some small way in its preparation.

Of course, you can't allow a regular diet of jam sarnies and baked beans, but you'll be amazed at how conventional children will become when given a free rein. Anarchy may rule for one menu, but they'll soon revert to more normal combinations.

Never, ever force-feed. You'll end up hating yourself, and your child will hate food. You can't help being anxious, but don't let it show. Do chat through mealtimes and avoid threats or bribery, but show pleasure at an almost clean plate. If you become really anxious, talk to your doctor or a dietary paediatrician.

Avoiding weight worries

Nowadays, many children become weight-conscious at an early age. If you have discussed the benefits and drawbacks of food from the beginning, it will be easy to discuss which foods are essential to health and fitness later on.

Don't arouse anxiety in your child by warning, 'You'll get fat,' but do be prepared to discuss worries with even quite small children who may become obsessed with fears about their appearance. If your child gets a balanced diet and plenty of physical activity, he should be fine. Avoid giving food to comfort your child in distress, as this can become a habit.

In the older child, a desire to over-eat may be a symptom of some worry or emotional disturbance. Don't call her greedy or deprive her of food. Instead, encourage her to talk about what is going on in her life so that you may address the real problem and allow the comfort eating to subside.

Your baby's health

When you first look at your new baby, a wave of panic can engulf you. How can something so small survive? And how can you cope with the enormity of caring for this fragile creature? Remember that babies were born and survived during the time of the caveman, of the Great Plague and a host of wars. They are tougher than you think, and today there is an army of professionals available to help when needed.

Trusting your instincts

Talk to your health visitor. Listen to the advice of friends, grandparents and professionals, but never underestimate your own instincts as a parent – particularly as a mother. If you think something is wrong, but someone who should know says all is well, weigh that opinion against your gut instinct. If you're still unhappy, ask for a second opinion. A leading paediatrician told me that he believes mothers do have an instinctive awareness of their children's condition, so don't be afraid to use it.

Safeguarding against cot death

The overwhelming majority of children survive and flourish. Cot death, which frightens so many new parents, occurs only rarely, and there are many ways in which you can safeguard against it.

Make sure your baby's room is warm but not too hot. Place her on her back to sleep and don't smother her in blankets – although blankets are better than a duvet. Never use a second-hand mattress. Her feet should be touching the bottom of the cot so that she can't wriggle under the blankets, and don't use a pillow until she is two years old. There may be times when you take your baby into your bed, but it's best to return her to her own cot to sleep. Be cautious about putting soft toys in the cot, and avoid exposing babies to cigarette smoke at all times. Be extra-vigilant if your baby seems at all unwell, and call a doctor if you feel uneasy. The risk of cot death exists between one month and five to six months.

Other conditions, such as hypothyroidism or phenylketonuria, will be detected by the thorough examination each child undergoes in the first week of life. If any adverse condition should be detected, then the appropriate treatment will be instituted at once, so if you work hand in hand with your obstetrician and health visitor, you shouldn't have any worries.

Teething

Most babies don't have their first tooth until they are around six months old – although it can be much later. Twenty milk teeth are already in the gums when your baby is born, and the process of them erupting through her gums can be painful.

She may salivate a lot and will want to chew anything in sight. Some babies develop a teething rash or looser bowels, but be careful of putting everything down to 'teething'. It could be some other condition that needs a doctor's attention.

To relieve some of your baby's discomfort, it may help to gently massage the gum area with a clean finger. Chemists can supply teething gels, but the most effective soother is something hard and cold for the baby to chew on.

Although milk teeth are temporary, (they loosen and fall out from the age of five), it is important to keep them free from decay, as they act as a foundation for healthy second teeth. Avoid sugary drinks and foods and institute good teeth-cleaning as a fun game. Use special children's toothpaste and let them copy your technique.

Always brush after children have eaten sweets, which can be given as a treat once a day. From the age of three or four, regular dental check-ups will help make your child feel comfortable with the dentist – and ensure that all is going well.

Preventing childhood diseases

As your child grows and starts to mix with other children and adults, he will come in contact with various infections. Some of these can be prevented by immunization (see chart on page 180).

Controversy over the MMR, or triple vaccine, causes anxiety for many parents. Some experts believe this injection against measles, mumps and rubella (German measles) is connected with autism. The vast majority of experts dispute this claim, and at present, the government recommends the triple vaccine for all children.

Not to immunize at all is foolish, because diseases like measles and polio can be life-threatening. If you have doubts, discuss them with your doctor. Having the injections separately is an option, but this can be expensive as the MMR triple jab is all that is on offer from the NHS. If you do opt to pay for single vaccines, it's vital to make sure you have all three administered. It is easy to have one or two and forget the third.

Coping with illness

If, in spite of all your precautions, your child falls ill, don't panic. Small children can be wan and prostrate one minute, running and shouting the next. Examine your child carefully for a rash. The meningitis rash will not disappear when a tumbler is rolled over the affected area. Other rashes will disappear and reappear when the pressure is lifted.

Sometimes illness will produce a wheezing cough or a rise in temperature. Be sure to keep heat-sensitive strips, which can be held against a child's forehead to read its temperature, in your first-aid box. Aching limbs, headaches, dizziness and confusion are other possible symptoms.

If you need to call out a doctor, it helps to have details of the symptoms you've noticed and the exact temperature. You'll get a quicker response if the doctor sees that you've taken sensible readings and are still alarmed. Saying, 'He seems hot, doctor,' isn't half as good as 'His temperature is 38°C (100°F).' Slight rises in temperature don't necessarily indicate serious illness.

Sponging the child's face and body with tepid water will lower a temperature. Never use cold water, and keep the child swaddled in towels or an absorbent cotton garment. It is vital to prevent your child from dehydrating, so give plenty of fluids. If these are refused because of a sore throat, keep on persuading, offering whatever drink appeals.

Never give a young child aspirin, which is dangerous in childhood, and go easy with paracetamol syrup. It's best to get a doctor or health visitor's advice before dosing your children. Don't worry too much about your child's lack of appetite at the height of a temperature or minor illness. Homemade soup, ice-cream, egg custard or any sloppy food has much more appeal than something which requires chewing.

Sometimes a childhood illness causes vomiting – not the gentle possetting of babies after a feed, but real sickness with retching and distress. If a child is persistently sick, he needs a doctor as soon as possible. If it's simply one bout of vomiting, be reassuring. Being sick is not pleasant, even for adults.

Once the episode is over, a quiet, darkened room with mum or dad nearby will calm a baby or young child. Try to emphasize that he'll soon be feeling better, and if possible, divert him with talk of tomorrow or some treat that lies ahead. It is important, too, to make sure he gets plenty of fluids to prevent dehydration, but stick to small sips at first, so as not to trigger another bout of retching.

Treating scrapes and abrasions

The small cuts and grazes that come from boisterous play need washing and then leaving open. Avoid antiseptic creams and solid plasters. If there must be a plaster dressing, pick a porous one that allows the skin underneath to breathe. If there's bleeding, press firmly on the wound with a clean pad. If the bleeding doesn't stop, get medical help.

Nosebleeds respond to pinching the nose firmly with finger and thumb applied just below the bridge.

Bee stings, nettles and burns

A few children are allergic to bee stings, so watch them carefully for a few hours. With stings, make sure any soothing cream you apply is suitable for children; some that include antihistamines are not.

When the inevitable moment comes that your child falls into a nettle patch, reach for the calamine lotion and avoid saying, 'Serves you right.' Children were made to explore.

Everywhere a small child goes should be screened for fire or heat danger, but if burns or scalds occur, then reduce the heat immediately by plunging the area into cold water. Don't apply ointments, which make the skin soggy and prone to infection. Don't prick blisters, however huge. They're there to prevent infection.

Choking and drowning

First-aid courses are invaluable for teaching the techniques to deal with choking. Babies should be held upside down by the legs and patted on the back. Older children should be bent over and slapped between the shoulder blades.

The technique of dislodging an object by standing behind and using clenched fists to deliver a sharp blow just below the victim's ribcage needs expert tuition, as does mouth-to-mouth resuscitation. If you arm yourself with a good knowledge of first-aid techniques, you'll feel more capable of dealing with emergencies.

If your child has swallowed a foreign object, take her immediately to an Accident and Emergency (A&E) unit. Difficulty in breathing, a suspicion that she's swallowed something noxious, or a fit or convulsion also need hospital treatment, and a severe fall or blow to the head needs a period of medical supervision.

Remember that a small child can drown in just an inch of water, so keep an eye on a child whenever water is near. This includes simple water sources such as buckets or ornamental fish-tanks.

Again, I must stress the importance of knowing how to deal with accidents involving water. If you can't teach your child to swim, take him to swimming lessons as soon as he's old enough to join.

Potty training

A healthy child senses when his bowels and bladder are emptying around the age of fifteen months, but he doesn't have sufficient muscle control to do anything about it. At eighteen months, you can begin to sit him on the potty after meals. Make this an enjoyable thing rather than a chore, and when he occasionally obliges, give lots of praise.

Be prepared for him to want to use the potty a lot (often without success) and discuss his successes with him. Never refer to failures. Gradually, they will become fewer, and by the age of two, he'll go all day without a nappy. At two-and-a-half, his night-time nappy is often dry, and by the age of three-and-a-half, he may well be happy to have a potty by the bed, or a light so that he can get to the toilet unaided.

Please don't start potty training too soon. An infant less than eighteen months old simply can't be trained, and it's cruel to try. After eighteen months, make sure he knows where his potty is, give him time without a nappy on – and above all, be patient.

Once a child is potty-trained, occasional bed-wetting may occur. This is best ignored unless it becomes frequent, at which time you need medical advice. Check, also, that your child is not under stress of any kind.

Dyslexia and dyspraxia

As your young child develops, you may notice things that cause anxiety. Perhaps he or she is bright enough in conversation, yet has difficulty in reading and writing. His skill with a ball may be less than that of his peers.

Don't immediately assume the worst. Lack of progress in reading can be an early sign of dyslexia, or it may be a hearing or sight impairment, yet it could also mean that a teacher has failed to motivate your child.

A child who has difficulty controlling a ball or whose work is untidy may have dyspraxia, a condition that used to be known as 'clumsy child syndrome'. It is due to interference with the signals coming from the brain to the organ concerned. It doesn't mean the child's intelligence is low. Both dyslexia and dyspraxia can be helped by therapy (see pages 184–7).

Left-handedness

Around one boy in ten and one girl in twelve is left-handed. A baby will show no preference for either hand. It's only towards the end of the second year that she will start to favour one hand, although she may switch allegiance after a while; you can't usually be sure that your child is left-handed until she reaches the age of three or four.

Being left-handed is *not* a disability. Trying to make your child right-handed can be damaging and lead to problems with speech and reading. Left-handed scissors should be freely available at nursery and school, and although extra effort is needed when learning to write, a left-handed child will soon catch up and be level with her right-handed peers.

Developmental problems

If you feel your child is not developing as fast as other children, talk to your health visitor, or if your child is at school, his teacher. Explain your fears and ask for opinions. Avoid letting the child know your anxieties or discussing his condition with everyone who comes to the house. Children should never feel that they are 'a problem'. If they have to go for treatment, be honest with them and be calm yourself. A small child gauges danger by how scared you are.

If your child is diagnosed as having a disability or disease, contact one of the helpful organizations listed on pages 184–7, so that you can be well-informed about the condition and whatever can be done to alleviate it. Don't be afraid to ask questions of doctors and therapists; they will understand your anxiety.

Be careful that the disability does not become the hub of family life. Do what you can to keep the family ticking over normally, and encourage your child to excel in other areas than those affected. If children have a problem to overcome, the more self-confident they are, the better.

Nervous habits

At some stage your child may develop a nervous habit such as twitching his nose, twiddling his hair, or grinding his teeth. It's best to ignore this at first, as it will probably pass quite quickly. If not, talk to your health visitor or doctor, but do avoid drawing attention to it. If a child finds that an action produces an audience, it's only natural that he should repeat the process.

Sleeping troubles

Nightmares, which usually begin at around age four, can be caused by unsuitable late-night snacks such as cheese or those with a high level of colourings and additives. Disturbing television programmes can lead to uneasy sleep, as can a worrying incident through the day.

Tell your child it was only a dream and stay with her until she is calm. Night terrors, an extreme form of nightmare, are rare, but frightening for both child and parent. In both cases, there is no need to worry unless they become regular occurrences, in which case seek expert help.

Pets

The latest research shows that living with a family pet can be beneficial to a child, but if the pet was already installed, be careful not to make it jealous. Don't appear for the first time with a child in your arms. Make a fuss of your pet and then introduce the baby.

A pet will want to sniff the newcomer, so hold its collar and let it sniff away, but avoid letting a pet lick your child or anything the child will handle or put to its mouth.

If you have a cat, use a cat net on your pram or cot because cats like to sleep near a warm bundle and could obstruct your baby's breathing – as well as such proximity being unhygienic. Talk to your veterinarian about keeping your pet healthy in order to protect the health of your child. However amiable your pet appears, never leave it alone with a small child.

PLAY

I almost called this section 'Friends' because friends are such an important part of play. However, I remembered those delicious moments of lone play that can stimulate your imagination or simply delight you, and so I settled for 'play' instead.

Parents and play

At the very beginning, a mother or father will play with a young child because he can't manage alone. But the tendency is to draw back once the child can handle toys and bricks. 'He's happily occupied,' parents think. 'I can get on with something else.' That's a pity, because research has shown that a parent's involvement can be beneficial, especially to young children.

Learning by imitation

Your child learns by watching your techniques with Lego™, dolly's buttons or poster paint, and his confidence increases. It's important, however, not to do things for your child all the time simply because you do them quicker or better, and never over-organize his play. Remember to offer a variety of toys if at all possible.

Jigsaws give great pleasure, but they are one-dimensional because they can only be played with in a way that leads to one conclusion. Building bricks can become roads or bridges, towers or train sets, and through them the child learns to use his imagination.

What about television?

Certainly, television can serve as a pleasant diversion for a child, but if it is allowed to become a child's only diversion, it is counter-productive. In addition, it can easily become a battleground as children compete to view their choice of programme.

This battleground, however, can provide an opportunity to practice fair play if you help your children schedule their viewing so that each gets his or her way some of the time. In addition, try to offer an alternative diversion to each child when it's his turn to surrender the remote control. If there's only one TV set, make sure mum and dad have their turns, too.

When to use censorship

Sometimes there may be programmes you'd prefer your children not to watch. Try to avoid openly prohibiting viewing, as this can arouse a desire that might not have existed before the ban. Instead, for younger children, try to plan some pleasurable family activity away from the screen.

With older children, of course, censorship is more difficult, as they may have access to TV elsewhere. With my own children, I eventually decided to content myself with expressing disapproval whenever I felt that a programme merited it and left it up to them to make a judgement.

Playing with others

Once your child is old enough to have playmates, he will begin to learn the value of cooperation. Although you must make sure that no child comes to physical harm, it's best to let your child learn from experience. If he shares, others will share with him. If he is dictatorial, his friends will turn away from him.

It is sometimes painful for a parent to stand back and watch a child negotiate the minefield of human relationships alone, yet the earlier that learning process begins, the happier your child will be.

Toys and stereotypes

Some parents are very disapproving of 'girl' or 'boy' toys. While it is true that it's damaging to stereotype the sexes, on the other hand, we should never force children to play with specific toys. Provide both varieties and let him or her choose.

Some experts believe boys are born with a predilection for aggression and girls with a leaning towards domesticity. My own view is that any such tendency is the result of generations of conditioning. Women were reared to be domesticated and 'nice'; men were brought up to be forceful and warlike. In a changed (and changing) world, we can now allow our children to be themselves, so if your son wants to play dolls' tea parties while your daughter disembowels a toy tractor, why not let them?

Toys of aggression

The same is true of aggressive toys. Telling your child that toy guns are forbidden will only make them unbelievably desirable. However, some studies have shown that aggressive toys do encourage more hostile behaviour among children. I suggest that, rather than ban them, you divert attention from them after a little while by proposing a more enjoyable and cooperative form of play. If this is vigorous and fun – for instance, a game of tag – the guns will soon be forgotten.

FRIENDS

Freedom should also apply to friendships. It's important to give your child access to other children whenever you can; this will lead to friendships.

If you don't like her choice of friend, ask yourself why. Unless real danger is involved, your child's choice should prevail – that's how she learns to judge character.

Imaginary friends

Don't be alarmed if, at some stage, your child develops one or more imaginary friends. Sometimes that imaginary friend can be a channel for displaying emotions.

For example, if your child tells you his imaginary friend is unhappy, that may be a way of introducing something he's embarrassed to talk about in relation to himself. If the imaginary friend has been naughty, that may mean he has been naughty and wants you to know it. There's no need for you to enter too far into the illusion; but don't simply dismiss it as 'silly'. It will pass in time.

General imaginative display usually emerges in the second year of life. A toddler will use any object to represent a car or a train, a cuddly toy becomes a mother or a child, he drinks from an imaginary cup or smacks his lips at imaginary food.

At the age of three, imagination extends to role-playing. He or she is a doctor one minute, a milkman the next, then a fireman. If there are some dressing-up clothes, an old handbag, shoes or cheap jewellery, they can role-play to their hearts' content.

Watching your child pretending to be you can often be a salutary experience! And allowing this kind of role-play frees your children to release aggressive impulses that might otherwise get them into trouble in a real-life situation.

CHILD CARE

Some mothers will want or need to go back to work when their babies are still quite young. There is a tendency to look upon child-minding as a modern phenomenon, but in fact, it began with the onset of the machine age. Today it is estimated that something like a quarter of a million children in this country are cared for by child-minders.

Some parents prefer to employ a nanny to work in their own home, but this can be expensive. Some couples opt for the father to become a full-time carer. This is a matter for individual decision, but it pays to consider the father's future when he is no longer needed in the home; in addition, his role as carer must not be secondary to the mother's role as breadwinner.

However, if both parents are happy with the arrangement this can be a rewarding situation. A father gets to know his child, and a mother has the peace of mind that comes from knowing her child is in the most loving of hands.

Choosing a child-minder

Before you leave your child with a child-minder or nanny, you need to know quite a lot about her no matter how highly recommended she is. Will your child be her sole charge or is she caring for other children? Is there enough space in her house and garden for all the children to play freely? What experience or training has she had? What equipment and play material does she provide? Does she set aside time to cuddle or read to each child? Above all, is her house clean and safe? What other adults will have access to the children because they live in her house? Does she offer a nourishing and attractive menu?

Under current legislation, someone who looks after a pre-school child in her own home for pay is required to be registered with the local authority, and this means she must conform to certain standards. However, that does not absolve parents from vigilance, or mean that the child-minder is without flaw.

Nannies

Only some of these questions apply to nannies. Parents will provide the safe and happy environment, but nannies' references need to be checked thoroughly. In time, a nanny may become almost a family member, but parents should still conduct spot-checks and listen carefully to what their child's words or behaviour tell them. Good nannies and child-minders will appreciate a parent who is interested enough to ask questions and carry out spot-checks.

In no circumstances leave your child with anyone he does not know well. Take time to make your child feel comfortable with the person who is going to take your place, even if this is a grandparent or aunt. There can be nothing more frightening for a child than to feel it has been abandoned with strangers or someone seen fleetingly the week before.

Discuss your requirements and standards with your nanny or child-minder. For instance, how do you want them to deal with naughtiness if it occurs? What about potty training or feeding habits? This is your child, so your will should prevail, but child-minders, and even doting grandmas, are not machines. They have standards and opinions, too, and the best way to sort this out is by cooperation.

Children learn by imitation, so it is inevitable that your child will pick up some of the habits and emotions of a person with whom she spends her day. That's why it is important to leave your child with someone of whom you fully approve. And a certificate or qualification doesn't necessarily mean that a person is right for your child.

Some mothers need to employ child-minders for school-age children. Try to find someone who is prepared to do more than just walk your child home from school and stick him in front of the TV. Although you will talk to your child later in the day, he may well need to unburden himself when school is over, and need a listening and sympathetic ear.

Nursery

When the time comes to find a nursery place, some of the same rules apply here as they do to choosing a child-minder. Sadly, there may not be a wide range of nurseries in your area, but shop around if you can. It's better to have a longer journey to nursery and a happy child than bring a weepy or sullen child home from just around the corner. You need to trust the staff, especially the person in charge, and you need to be frank with her about anything in the home which may upset your child.

Your child also needs to know that the two adults who control his or her life are cooperating, especially over matters such as feeding and lavatory training. A good nursery staff will not simply 'mind' the children in their care; they will stimulate them and prepare them to enjoy being part of a group. They should also talk to the children, encouraging conversation and ensuring that the youngsters can talk freely about anything that troubles them.

3

how to have a happy child

All too soon, it seems, your 'baby' becomes ready to take her first steps away from you. Primary school looms, but how do you decide which one is best for your child? For a start, all local education authorities publish a list of schools in their area, and you should be able to find these at your civic centre or library.

Try to check out several schools, because you may find that your first choice can't or won't take your child. Also, beware of leaving the choice of a school until the last minute; it's much better to allow at least a year for the process. Schools will tell you when they are having an open day. Most head teachers welcome enquiries. If they don't, then you need to ask yourself why.

Choosing the right school

When you visit a prospective school, look closely at the work on display. Is it the work of the children or is it 'show' work put there by teachers? If it is children's work, is it full of expression and a sense of freedom? These are the qualities you should hope to find in the children themselves.

Ask what sort of parental involvement there is and whether or not the school has an anti-bullying policy. If the answers to these two questions are vague, you should be concerned.

Government reports

These days, we tend to hear rather a lot of information about government performance tables and Ofsted reports. Certainly, a wise parent will study these, but there is no substitute for parental inspection. Also, be sure to listen to your child. He or she will have an opinion, and should get to know the school well before going.

Make sure your child understands the school set-up. Visit as often as is necessary so that she knows the layout. It's important that she knows how to do up buttons and has shoes she can take off or fasten herself.

Put her name on her possessions and make sure she knows some of the children who will be her new playmates. She should be able to go to the lavatory herself, identify her own name and be prepared to listen attentively.

The first day

Prepare beforehand for the first day at nursery or school. Your child will pick up on your vibes. If you seem to think it's going to be good, then she will probably think so, too.

Talk about the things you saw at the school when you visited it together, and be calm and relaxed. Discuss how you'll be eager to hear all the news when she gets home, and plan a little treat to celebrate such a momentous day.

If possible, arrange for your child to meet another child she knows when you take her to school on the first day, and try not to hang around, even if she appears to be upset.

Trust the staff to calm her fears and draw her into activities. She can do this more easily if you're not there to cling to.

If your child seems very upset, stay outside for ten minutes and then creep back. You'll probably glimpse your son or daughter absorbed in some activity and over the tears, but make sure you're not seen.

Is your child gifted?

We all think our children are the most wonderful ever, but a few parents may feel they have a gifted child.

Although giftedness may not manifest itself early, there are some early signs. Gifted children may attain bowel and bladder control early, walk and talk sooner than the average and develop an extensive vocabulary. They may have extra energy and need less sleep (although this can also be a characteristic of hyperactivity).

They exhibit an insatiable curiosity. They may be extra-observant and also have the ability to reason. Their imagination may be vivid and their memory retentive. For all these reasons, they often prefer the company of adults or older children because this provides a challenge.

It's important to remember that a child who has had a lot of attention may be advanced in some of these ways, but may not be necessarily extra-gifted. Although children should always be provided with play material that challenges their abilities, it's best not to try and 'hothouse' them or indulge in too many daydreams about their future. If they're happy and interested in the world around them, that's enough for the moment.

Holidays

School holidays can be either six weeks of bliss or an equal amount of nightmare, so be sure to prepare carefully for them. Having a 'treat' day each week will ensure better behaviour the rest of the time, and if you can rope in aunts or grandpas to give you a day off, then that's a bonus.

If you can, arrange an activity for the long break. Redesigning a bedroom or playroom or changing something in the garden can give a sense of purpose and achievement to those long summer weeks.

Behaviour

A parent who wants to keep his or her sanity needs a sense of humour. The difficulty is knowing when to see the funny side of something and when it needs to be taken seriously. When a disaster occurs – the breaking of a precious ornament, for example – a child has been punished enough by the shock of the incident. If it happened in spite of repeated warnings, however, you might ask him to pay for it out of his pocket money.

Pocket money

Pocket money can be an important tool in accepting the realities of life – although no matter how much you give, you will probably be told someone else's parents give more. How much you allow your child depends on your circumstances, but take into account what other parents are providing and don't give huge amounts more.

If you can't afford the 'going rate', be

honest with your children. Most children understand simple economics from an early age; if you can't keep up with other parents, they'll appreciate your honesty and your efforts to provide them with what you can. Pocket money can be given as soon as a child is old enough to understand spending, but the amount given then should be small.

Encourage your children to save some pocket money, but don't ask too much of them – and be prepared for them to squander a bit now and then. This is how they learn. Don't fall into the trap of using deprivation of pocket money as a regular means of discipline. You'll feel mean and your children will feel badly done by. It also means that you could be punishing your child on pocket-money days, a week after the offence occurred. If what he did wrong was important, this is probably all right, but if fining him becomes routine, the punishment loses meaning.

Bribes and treats

Similarly, using money as a bribe to ensure good behaviour is counter-productive. It encourages a feeling that normal behaviour should be rewarded. Resist the temptation to say, 'If you'll be good, I'll give you…' Instead, occasionally say, 'You've been very good lately so I think we might go to…' and name somewhere your child likes to go.

Be careful, however, not to give out treats too lavishly, because this can encourage your child to lobby constantly for more! It's understandable that they should do this if they feel their efforts will be successful, so never reward whinging, however much you may long for peace. A child who whinges is either anxious or unhappy and needs attention – or has been led to believe that whinging pays!

Tale-telling

Another form of whinging is tale-telling. Now no one likes a sneak, but in a small child, tale-telling may have a purpose other than just being mean. Your child may be testing your standards. 'Jane's just taken a sweet,' may mean 'Is it all right if I take one, or will you be cross?' Persistent tale-telling can be a sign of deep insecurity or fear of what may happen. All too often, the child's need is ignored as it is told not to be a tale-teller.

Attention-seeking behaviour

Young children may go through a phase of attention-seeking and this can be wearing. They seem to have an inbuilt gauge that tells them exactly when to push your buttons and drive you to the end of your tether. When this happens, try to understand what is happening. Did you give her extra attention the first time she made a play for notice? If so, you are getting a learned response.

Most children crave the attention of the people they love best: their parents. If you only give your children attention when they are naughty, then you can be certain that they'll be naughty. Start to give attention spontaneously, and for no reason other than that they are playing nicely or in a quiet mood. Once this is in place, ignore the attention-seeking by walking away to do something else; don't sit there coldly like a brick wall. Simply go off to wash up or cook or tidy a room.

Unless it's dangerous, don't reprove any form of attention-seeking, because reproof or punishment is, in a strange way, giving the attention the child wanted. If you lose your cool and scream, that can also seem like attention. So don't react with anger, however tempted you may be. This isn't easy, but if you stick to it, it will pay dividends.

Swearing

Two things that distress parents are the use of bad language and answering back. Remember that, although children know this is naughty, they don't have an adult concept of what they're doing. 'Being cheeky' quite probably elicited a laugh the first time it happened because you were taken by surprise. Similarly, a word that causes you to jump immediately goes into your child's armoury. Show horror at the word 'chair' and a small child will regard it as swear word of the week!

Swearing, in a small child, has to be learned behaviour, and sometimes parents catch an uncanny echo of their own speech patterns. If your five-year-old says, 'I'm bloody fed up with this,' he didn't learn it from a nursery rhyme. With a small child, it's probably best to ignore the odd oath – although you should find out where they are being picked up.

With older children, explain that swearing is not a good idea because it's something people with a limited vocabulary are forced to do. If you should happen to swear inadvertently, tell them you don't feel proud of it. If you can give the impression that swearing is uncool and not something that sends you into a frenzy, that may be the end of it. If not, in older children, let them see that swearing in the presence of children and adults is not behaviour calculated to bring approval. And never tell them they shouldn't do it because they're children. This suggests that swearing is an adult privilege and therefore infinitely desirable.

Cheekiness

'Being cheeky' can be satisfying for a child who feels frustrated and hard done by. It's most likely to occur when a child thinks he's not being listened to or allowed to have a point of view. It's sure to recur if he sees it makes you smile! Don't respond to insolence but try not to make a big deal out of it. Say 'We'll talk when you calm down,' and move away. But be sure to keep your promise to talk and to listen. If your child learns which type of language and tone brings results, he'll adjust.

A child who obeys your every command without argument is simply giving you blind obedience and is not thinking things through for herself, so try not to feel threatened by argument or failure to obey immediately. You have the benefit of experience; you know what is right. Your child has to learn, and if questioning is seen as insolence, or at best, awkwardness, she will never learn. Of course, when your child responds to a request with 'Why?' it's a temptation to say 'Because I say so.' But that's an unproductive response. Explain why and you should get more cooperation.

When your child asks for something or permission to do something, try not to give a flat 'No'. Instead, say 'I'm sorry, we can't do that now, but perhaps we can tomorrow.' If it's an impossibility, suggest an alternative. If it's a request for something dangerous or beyond your means, explain why it can't be done. If you treat your child with respect, he'll react more responsibly.

I realize that this is the counsel of perfection. Driven to distraction, you may want to take your offspring by the throat. But remember: *you* are the one with the power – and your children know it. They can feel vulnerable and often powerless, so use your superiority carefully. If they never win, they will either wind up wanting to lash out, or unable to hold their own in the outside world.

Although you have always to respect your child's individuality and rights, there will be times when, faced with a defiant child, your will has to prevail. It's best to avoid head-on confrontations. Instead, say, 'I'm sorry. That isn't going to happen,' and then walk away. If he threatens to go ahead anyway, deprive him of the opportunity to do whatever is in contention but don't harangue or threaten. It's important that you are sure of your own superior authority if you are to convince your child of it – so don't hammer it home.

When the episode is over, behave normally. Don't relish your triumph or feel the need to compensate them for losing. It's over now and best forgotten.

Arguments

Family arguments are an essential training ground for life. If you cannot engage in argument in the safety of the family, how can you know how to argue in the outside world? The parent who is willing to let an argument run without using parental authority to curtail it is training a child for the future.

This training can begin at a very early stage. When your toddler insists on wearing her summer T-shirt in December, let her. Take along a warm cover-up to produce when she shivers, but don't say, 'I told you so.' Next time, when you say, 'It's cold outside,' she'll believe you and opt for a sweater.

Tantrums

Tantrums can be a feature of early childhood. Sometimes a toddler will hold his breath until a parent panics. This usually begins at around eighteen months. A two-year-old knows what he wants and needs to do, but something (sometimes you, sometimes his own lack of capability) is stopping him. Anger erupts into fury, and the child stops breathing. His face turns blue as the air supply diminishes. It's a terrifying sight, but the moment the child faints for lack of oxygen, his tongue muscles relax and he will breathe again.

Remember that your child is as terrified as you are of these uncontrollable emotions. Reaching out to give a gentle cuddle can stop things coming to a head. Children outgrow breath-holding, and if you handle them carefully, the tantrums will cease. See them for what they are: attempts to make your child's world the way he wants it to be. That may be annoying for you, but it's logical on his part to try to make things work out his way.

Avoid tantrums by never saying 'No' unreasonably. For your child to feel safe, 'No' must mean 'No' and never 'Maybe.' To say 'No' and then give in to a temper tantrum is re-enforcing the idea that being naughty pays dividends. I know you love your child to bits, and seeing him distressed is painful. But if you really love him, you'll help him to realize that bad behaviour doesn't pay. If you give in to a tantrum, you teach him that 'No' means 'Yes, but you must have a tantrum first.'

Avoid situations that may lead to tantrums. Your voice can be helpful here. 'Firm but loving' is what you should aim for. If you speak pleasantly but with enough conviction, you signal that tantrums will be a waste of time. Use diversion, too. Suggest a game or a walk, anything to take your toddler's mind off trouble. This is especially helpful later in the day, because tiredness is a frequent cause of tantrums.

Don't forget cuddles. A tired child contemplating defiance will often melt in a warm embrace and decide not to bother after all. Once in a tantrum, your child needs you to be calm. Sit down beside him to make sure he doesn't hurt himself, but don't intervene unless you have to for safety reasons.

When it subsides, say something quite unrelated. 'Shall we go and look for daddy? or 'Will you help me sort these buttons?' will be more productive than 'We don't want any more of that, do we?' Of course, this kind of restraint is difficult when you may be in need of a cuddle yourself. That's the time to remember that you are grown up and a parent to boot – and saintliness comes with the territory.

Bullying

No one likes a bully, but bullies are children, too, and it's important to work out a bully's motivation. Is he copying behaviour he sees in you and simply trying to get his own way?

Is some other frustration or unhappiness leading to him becoming aggressive with his peers or younger children? Or is he afraid that he is failing at something and trying to prove himself in other ways? Very few children bully for pleasure. If they do, they need the kind of specialist help school psychologists can provide.

If your child is a victim of bullying, it is important that you react in a sympathetic manner, but don't immediately say that you will confront the bully. This will make your child afraid of retribution and unwilling to come to you again.

Discuss the level of the problem. Can it be dealt with by walking away? Is it simply words which, however hurtful, can be ignored? Helping your child to rise above teasing is very worthwhile.

However, if the bullying is aggressive or designed to humiliate, then you need to act. Persuade your child to allow you to talk to the grown-ups concerned at nursery or school. Most schools have an anti-bullying policy, but all schools should cooperate with parents to stamp out bullying.

Bedtime

Bedtimes can be battlegrounds, especially when your child is tired but determined to win another half hour just to prove he or she can. It's natural for a child to want to stay where there's conversation and interest, but sleep is important, so you need to establish some rules.

I believe in routine but not in inflexibility. Turning off the TV five minutes before the end of a well-loved programme won't make for a restful night. Saying that there isn't time for a story because it's one minute to deadline seems mean. You must guard against the gradual erosion of bedtime, but don't feel that your authority is at risk if you allow an extra five minutes now and then.

Small children like being tucked in and kissed goodnight, but if they're not tired it's better to let them sit in their cot with a well-loved toy or picture book. Go back in half an hour when they're asleep, and you can remove the toy and tuck them in for the night. Older children may enjoy half an hour to read or listen to music.

However you play it, make bedtimes happy times. And never allow a child who has been put to bed to come back into the bosom of the family. Allow it once and it will be that child's constant aim in future. If she needs reassurance after a dream or a scare, go to her rather than have her come to you.

Polite society

We all want our children to be polite, partly because we want to be proud of them, but mainly because politeness will ease their passage through life. The best way to instil politeness in children is to set an example. If you are polite to them, they will respond; as they respond to you, so will they behave with others. Encourage them to be respectful of the old and protective of the young. Whether or not you're an animal-lover, show a reverence for all life. From such things is politeness born.

It's nice to see children behaving graciously, but beware of expecting too much too soon. A small child, offered a plate of cake, will study the size of portions and opt for the largest slice. This is normal behaviour. At that age, it's logical to put your own interests first. In time, as he comes to enjoy sharing, he will become generous. If your behaviour towards him is generous he will see this as an adult and superior way to be.

Stealing

Some forms of behaviour are more important than simple manners. Stealing and overtly sexual behaviour trouble parents greatly. A child of three or less does not fully understand ownership. He may get upset when a friend purloins one of his toys, but will happily bring home someone else's toy car. This action has no malicious intent, and it is important to realize this. 'Jamie will miss his car,' is all you need to say, because that is a concept your child can grasp. He will return it because it makes sense to soothe Jamie's distress.

At five or so, a child understands that stealing is wrong, but he has a strong sense of his own needs. If a friend has a bag of sweets and he has none, it seems natural to redress the balance. You have to explain possession and point out that what is his is his, and he wouldn't like to lose it. So it is for everyone.

A one-off theft is not the slippery slope to gangsterdom, but persistent pilfering is a cause for concern; it can be a sign of some underlying emotional problem. A child who feels deprived of love or attention may steal because the possession of the stolen property seems somehow fair in the face of his deprivation; it is also comforting. Punishing a child in this situation is counter-productive. Seek specialist help (see pages 184–7).

Lying

Lying tends to get some parents into a lather, as many are convinced that it is a sign of moral turpitude. Very young children don't lie consciously; they have difficulty in distinguishing fantasy from reality. Most small children will lie if they sense they are in trouble, even when they've been caught red-handed. It is usually only after the age of three or four that a child develops moral awareness and knows what a lie is. If you severely punish lying, the likelihood is that your child will simply try to lie more effectively next time.

Lies that are in fact exaggerations – for example, lying about family wealth or achievement – are generally harmless, but they may indicate a lack of confidence in the importance of a child's own reality. In this instance, boosting your child's confidence is more important than punishment.

The imaginative lie – 'There's a witch in the wardrobe' – isn't a lie at all and should be treated as the play-acting it is. And explain white lies to your child if you use them yourself. She'll understand the need not to hurt someone's feelings. Above all, explain why lies are counter-productive. Never, ever threaten to withdraw your love.

The child who lies is simply trying to ease her path through life. Helping her to do this in other ways will have better results. If you feel the need to punish, however, make sure that the punishment is reasonable.

Sexual curiosity

Sexual curiosity is natural in a small child. Remember that, to a child of two or three, a penis is no more or less interesting than a nose or an ear.

Boys of pre-school age can have erections and derive some satisfaction from what they see as a phenomenon, but this is not a sexual act to a child. His body is simply changing before his eyes. This is interesting, but it is certainly not erotic.

Fifty per cent of children under five engage in genital handling, and some children masturbate. Parents find this embarrassing because they see it as sexual behaviour, but in fact, the child derives comfort from it, not sexual stimulation. It equates with thumb-sucking in that it is soothing. Your child will only begin to attach sexual connections if it sees that you are alarmed and disturbed by this particular action.

Don't exhibit anger or punish him if you see him masturbating. Ask him gently not to do it and then change the subject by providing a diversion. If you don't succeed and your child becomes preoccupied with sexual handling, consult an expert, because this can be a sign of stress.

The average seven-year-old will fall about when breasts, penises and bottoms are mentioned. This laughter is healthy and if you can react in a calm way, you do much to ensure a healthy sexual attitude in your child in later years.

Smacking

It is impossible to discuss behaviour without referring to smacking. Some experts would like to see smacking made illegal. I don't agree with that view because I think it would inevitably lead to the courts intervening in family life just because good mums or dads lost their temper once in public and found themselves in trouble. This would benefit no one, certainly not a child. But that doesn't mean I approve of smacking. A child who is habitually smacked or beaten is the victim of abuse, for which there are existing legal constraints.

If you smack your child because she smacked her brother, you confuse her. He annoyed her, so she smacked him; she annoyed you, so you smacked her. Where's the difference? Smacking also diminishes a child's sense of guilt over a wrong action. She feels she has 'paid the price', so it's OK. If you smack, you may encourage your child to lie his way out of trouble. Also, never smack your child for what you see as a 'sexual' offence, such as masturbation or sexual curiosity. That only links sex with punishment in the child's mind, and this can be damaging in later life.

Although I don't think a well-loved child is doomed because mum or dad once tap his bottom when he runs into the road or throws his sister's favourite toy into the loo, I do think smacking should be avoided. Instead, explain why such actions are wrong. He may get run over! How would he feel if his sister disposed of his toy? Find other ways of punishing him if you must, but never withdraw your love. And never give dire warnings of punishments you both know you'll never carry out. What you threaten, you must do, so think first.

Trying to understand your child's thought processes is the key to dealing with behaviour. Don't set impossible standards, whether its over tidying his room or playing with friends.

Decide where you need to make a stand and where you should turn a blind eye. If you constantly chide your child he will cease to listen. If your complaints are rare, you'll receive maximum attention. Don't issue ultimatums unless you mean them. When you do, you must carry out your threat. But beware of breaking that small spirit that is your offspring. Very few offences merit that.

SAFETY ISSUES

In order for your children to feel secure, they must have confidence in their own ability to cope in some difficult situations. They can't have this confidence unless you have allowed it to develop.

This means standing back, biting your tongue, while they learn by trial and error. Your wanting to protect them is entirely natural; you are programmed to feel that way. But just as you must not help the chick out of the egg, so you must draw back from too much cosseting of your child.

Advance preparation

In order to have peace of mind for yourself, prepare in advance. Teach your child road safety and enquire whether or not your local police force runs any kind of safety schemes. Make sure that whenever he is away from you, he knows where you are, knows his own name, address and telephone number.

Of course, a very young child will never be away from you unless it is in the prearranged care of someone you trust, but children can and do get lost in crowded stores, at sporting events, funfairs or in other situations involving lots of people. Tell them that, if they do happen to get lost, they should stand still and wait for you to find them rather than stray further in search of you. If they are old enough, tell them to go to the nearest ticket office or to ask someone serving at a counter or at a cash register to help.

Of course, it is vital that children trust police officers, but small children may not be able to distinguish between one uniform and another, so this instruction must be approached with caution. Warn them not to go with anyone, however friendly they may seem, but instead, to ask the grown-up to find you and bring you back to them.

And above all, make sure that they stand still in a place where there are lots of people milling around.

Dealing with strangers

It is important to stress that strangers in cars are to be avoided, but much child molestation is carried out by people known to the child, so don't overplay the 'wicked stranger' theme. Give them a back-up source of help, such as grandma's phone number, and tell them that no friendly adult who says they've come on mum's behalf will mind if they check first. Some parents use a family password, but if this should get into the wrong hands, it can give a child a false sense of security.

Explaining to children that there are people who might harm them is difficult, but in this day and age, it can't be shirked. Even so, try to avoid giving the impression that the world is full of monsters waiting to do terrible things to children.

I told my son that there were a few sad people who might want to steal him away to live with them. He wouldn't like this, we would positively hate it, and therefore we must make sure it never happened. This approach made him cautious but not apprehensive of every stranger he met. It also has the advantage of not depicting abductors as 'wicked-looking' people – something which can make a child vulnerable to a predator who happens to look 'nice'.

News reports

Given the amount of media that bombards us everyday, it is virtually impossible for children to avoid hearing news reports of child murder or abduction. Yet hourly news bulletins on missing children can be quite worrying for a child, and his or her fears need to be addressed. Be honest, but don't overwhelm him with the truth. Yes, a child is missing. Yes, something may have happened to it, but such things happen rarely.

If you are asked whether the child may be dead, say 'Yes,' but emphasize that there is always hope of a better outcome. If bad news does come eventually, be prepared to talk about it, emphasizing that such a sad episode happens one time in a million, and then try some diversion tactics.

While disturbing on one hand, such a conversation does allow you to stress the importance of not straying, of always keeping in touch with home and staying with playmates, but do this with a light touch.

The aim is to warn, not terrify. No child of primary-school age should be far from home without adult supervision and rigid return times.

In all situations, talk to other mothers. Cooperation between parents can prevent your children playing the game of 'Everyone else's mummy lets them'. It helps, too, to cooperate in activities such as collecting children from classes, parties or from group meetings like brownies or cubs.

Keeping the channels open

The greatest safety factor of all, in my opinion, is easy communication with your children. If, when they tell you they came close to danger, you throw a blue fit, they'll soon learn not to tell you things you may really need to know. They need to be able to confide in you without being mocked.

If they tell you they don't like a certain adult, don't ignore them or tell them not to be silly. Trust their instincts and talk it through with them. It may be a simple case of a child taking offence at a reprimand. Or it could be that they feel someone is touching them inappropriately or speaking suggestively and they need to feel free to tell you, their protector. Trust like that has to be built up over time.

Never say 'You always seem to be in trouble' or 'You and your imagination'. Such simple remarks can seal your children's lips at the wrong time. Remind them of your ability to protect them no matter what threats are made against them, and convince them that the whole of society – police, teachers, other parents – would be on their side if abuse occurred.

The child who can communicate freely with her parent wears a shield against abuse of all types.

Defining sexual abuse

It can be difficult to define sexual abuse. Children sometimes play 'doctor and nurse' games that are born more out of normal curiosity than sexual urge.

The Royal College of Psychiatrists defines child sexual abuse as any 'sexually inappropriate act involving a child which is committed by a person five or more years older'. In other words, 'doctors and nurses' acted out by a five- and seven-year-old may need to be gently discouraged, but does not constitute abuse.

However, where a child under five is involved, it is regarded as abuse because the youngster cannot be said to have entered into the play willingly.

Of course, you must interpret a situation in your own way, and there are helpful organizations listed on pages 184–7 to whom you can turn for support. True sexual abuse, however, is a serious matter and should always be reported.

TRUTH ISSUES

One of the most difficult decisions you will face as a parent is when to tell your child the truth. I believe you should never lie, because once caught out, your child will never trust your word again.

However, it's usually not necessary to deluge children with every detail of the truth. When they ask about items in the news that distress them, be prepared to discuss, but point out that bad things occur rarely and are unlikely to happen to them. This is a good opportunity to state why there are rules about playing outside and coming home or staying close in crowds. Once you're sure they're satisfied, take their minds off the subject with a diversion, but never distract them at the beginning. They know they're being fobbed off, and that only increases their fears.

Children are acutely aware of tensions in the home, so, if you know they've heard a marital row, be honest. Saying, 'Yes, I'm cross with Daddy, but I still love him' is reassuring. Saying, 'Don't be silly. There's nothing wrong' is not.

Visits to the doctor or dentist are another area where being truthful is difficult. I had vowed never to lie to my son, but saying 'Yes, the injection may hurt a little bit,' wasn't easy. The benefit was that when I said 'This won't hurt at all,' I was believed.

Praising your children is vital, but keep the praise within the realms of truth. Telling them something they've done is perfect when it is not is as counter-productive as constantly running them down. Be constructive in both praise and criticism and they'll come to value your opinion.

Censorship

Television sometimes displays images that are difficult for a child to cope with. Try to anticipate when there are programmes you don't want your children to see. Don't announce, 'You're not seeing that,' but arrange some diversion to keep them away from the screen.

If something appears that you think may scare or puzzle your children, don't immediately switch off and change the subject. Discuss what they've seen and allow them to give their views. Too strict censorship leads to children trying to see programmes elsewhere. Use your judgement to protect your children from the media while at the same time allowing them to enjoy the benefits it can offer.

Moods

Accept that your child may sometimes feel fed up. It helps to be honest about your own moods. Unless you're a superb actor, you won't be able to hide how you feel, so it is better to say 'I feel a little miserable today because…' and then enlist their help to cheer you up. If you are worried about something, then explain, but keep it in proportion. Stress the actions you can take if the worst happens. This not only calms their fears, but it encourages them to look for coping strategies themselves.

Remember that almost nothing you can tell your children can be as bad as the image they conjure up in their imaginations. Be truthful and trust your instincts in knowing how far to go.

TALKING ABOUT SEX

If you've begun sex education early enough, you should have no difficulty in giving truthful answers to your children's questions as they grow. The school playground will abound with sexual untruths. They need you to give them facts in a context of family life and sensible behaviour.

This is not encouraging experimentation or arousing curiosity that would otherwise be dormant; it's responding to the needs of your growing children and equipping them for the dangers and temptations of adolescence. If you feel ill-equipped to deal with sex education, consult your local library. You should find all the information you need there, but relating the facts to your own experience and stressing the need to make sexual relationships important and meaningful is as important as explaining the mechanics of contraception.

I believe sex education should begin in

infancy. Telling your baby how much you loved carrying him or her inside you before birth is laying the foundations. A small child will accept that a baby needs to be kept safe, and where better than a mother's tummy?

Let your child see a newborn and explain that it needed protection and grew from an egg until it was big enough to emerge. If the next question is 'How did it get out?' explain. The truth will do: that a mother's body has a special place which expands when it is needed and thus allows the baby to be born.

Use proper names like 'vagina' if you're happy with them. The trick is to remember that you're explaining a miracle, so let your enthusiasm show. To a child, there is nothing 'dirty' about sex or birth. We infect children with our prurience as they grow, so describe the functions of a mother's body in pregnancy as you would explain a sneeze or bending and stretching. They are all natural processes.

How much to tell

It is extremely unlikely that a question about conception will follow immediately. It will come eventually, but try not to anticipate it. When you do have to answer it, remember to explain that it, too, is a natural process, but one that should belong to adulthood.

Explain the importance of preparing a home, or a 'nest', for the baby before conception. Explain how you and your partner (or you alone, if you are single), looked forward and made sure that you had a safe place for a baby. Adoptive parents can explain their longing and how hard they searched to find the right child to love.

Emphasize that the making of a baby is a loving action between grown-ups. It can be a joyful experience to see a child absorb this knowledge – almost gleefully because that is how they came to be and that's a good feeling. If you're a single parent with an absent father, explain that conception came out of love, but then you went your separate ways.

In sexual matters, as in everything else, don't give an untrue answer you will have to retract, such as 'You were found under a gooseberry bush.' It will cause complications for you, and it isn't fair on your child.

RELATIONSHIPS

Joyful family gatherings linger in the memory and can be a rich part of our life experience. But family life can also be a minefield. For every parent who craves the help and involvement of grandparents, there are others who see such involvement as interference or a refusal to let them assume their proper parental status.

Grandparents

Each family must make up its own rules about the role of grandparents, but if possible, such a role should exist. For some grandparents, the new birth can seem like a chance to be parents again. They experience the same level of wonder and joy they felt at the birth of their own children, but this time they have knowledge and experience they didn't possess then. It's not surprising, therefore, that they may be tempted to interfere. To a new parent, such interference may at first be comforting – but be careful. A child should only have one set of parents, and too much intervention, however well-meant, can undermine the fragile confidence of the new parent.

Whatever the difficulties, the advantages of a good grandparent-child relationship far outweigh the disadvantages. Even after divorce, it's best to keep up links with both sets of grandparents. They are part of the mosaic that is your child's life. It is a pity to have missing pieces, unless family friction rules out the possibility.

One of the most important responsibilities of parents and grandparents alike is to ensure that the child they love can go happily out into life. Spoiling a child is self-indulgent, and ultimately harmful. Children who know that gran will countermand mum's rule, or that their own parents will bend to their will, expect that kind of treatment at school and later in life. When the world isn't so forthcoming, these children feel rejected, and considerable emotional damage can ensue.

This applies not only to treats or breaking rules; it also applies to conversation. Children love attention, especially from a parent. A toddler who wants to impart some fresh information will take his mother's face in his hands and physically turn it away from whoever she is talking to in order to possess her full attention.

No one wants to discourage a child's communication, but saying, 'In a minute, darling,' and finishing your conversation will let him see that he must take his turn for attention. It's vital, however, that as soon as possible, you do turn to him. That teaches him that waiting politely pays off.

Sibling rivalry

The feeling that your brother or sister is really the advantaged one occurs to every child at some stage. 'She always gets more than me' or 'You let him get away with anything' are common cries. Rows over who goes at what time are the accompaniment to many bedtimes. The eldest child frequently feels put-upon; the youngest child resents being the baby of the family; middle children struggle to establish a place.

This can be painful for parents, but accept it as part of family life. Listen to all those cries of 'It's not fair!' in case there's a grain of truth in them. Answer reasonably. 'He doesn't have to wash up because he's too young to handle crockery' will produce a better response than 'Because I say so.'

Be careful over bedtimes. Sending an eleven-year-old to bed early because the five-year-old won't go without him is simply unfair. Yet each child should be helped to realize that along with their privileges go responsibilities. The older child stays up later, but he also has chores; the younger child, who goes to bed earlier, doesn't have to carry out household tasks. And each child should have a turn to feel important. Too often, the eldest child becomes a parent's confidant, leaving the other children outside the magic 'adult' circle.

Making comparisons can fuel sibling rivalry. However much you might like child number two to be like child number one, don't let those words pass your lips. Nor should you expect your child to follow a family tradition. Going to university to pursue the career of your choice is one thing; doing it only because 'Everyone in our family goes to university' is sad.

Be scrupulously fair about sharing out treats. Boys are often as clothes-conscious as girls and should have their fair share of the clothing budget.

Although it's important to be even-handed with your children, you must also be aware of differing needs. One child may need lots of cuddling, another may not. Try to give to each what is needed. This is not showing favouritism; it's accepting your children as individuals. And because they're individuals, they need their own time with you. This can be difficult, especially if you're a working mum, but it is never impossible. Take one child when you do the supermarket run. By listening on the journey there, you'll learn more than in hours of group conversation. Make separate bathtimes with younger children, or have one of them help you in the kitchen. And praise each child's achievements whenever you can.

Above all, recognize that your children are lucky to be part of a family. It's natural that there will be jealousy sometimes or feelings of resentment, but learning how to control these feelings within the family is wonderful preparation for life in the outside world.

Confidence

Initially in the home and then at school, children must find their own place. Some children have a natural impulse towards self-assertion. Others are almost afraid to take a leading role. Some of this second group will become bossy in an effort to establish some sort of control over the situation they fear. It's best to leave children to sort out these situations, but be watchful.

The naturally assertive child may need help to understand the desires and needs of others; the self-effacing child may need his confidence boosted; and the 'bossy' child needs to feel safe in his world. All these interventions should be subtle, and if possible, made away from the scene.

Talking to your child during bathtime or while walking in the park and discussing what goes on in group play is more helpful than wading in at play and telling Johnny to pipe down and Jennifer to stick up for herself.

In stressful situations, making eye contact with your child can be helpful. It signals, 'It's OK. I'm here but you can cope.'

In all situations, remember that your child is an individual. What he or she needs from a situation may not be what *you* would want in that situation. Your child must grow and develop his or her own potential. He can never be a second chance to realize an unfulfilled ambition for you or for grandparents.

If this achievement of potential is to come about, your child must learn to make choices from an early age. Of course, you must apply common sense if safety is involved, or if the choice made could have irrevocable consequences, but in most other matters, children can be allowed to decide for themselves.

Like every mother, I've hovered, terrified my children would be hurt or humiliated, but I've tried to let them do their own thing whenever possible – even when I knew it might have disadvantages.

A new baby

A new arrival can unsettle a first-born who's been used to having mum and dad to herself. A young child may think, 'Does that mean they've tired of me?' It's as well to delay telling her a baby is on the way, because to a child, nine months is forever. But tell her before she's likely to hear it in conversation or in whispered asides, or before your tummy is big enough to push her off your knee.

Once the baby is born, make sure visitors speak to her before they speak to the baby. Have a present for her to give the baby and one for the baby to return. Make changes in her routine that emphasize her importance. A few minutes later at bedtime, time to spend with mum and dad while the baby sleeps... such little things can ease doubts that she's being supplanted. And let her help with the baby chores of nappy-changing and bathtime.

A child's position in the family can influence personality. A second-born can feel constantly behind a first-born, especially if that first-born is clever or gifted. A middle child can feel 'nowhere' compared to being the eldest or the spoiled 'baby' of the family. Wise parents avoid such pitfalls by seeing their children as individuals and making sure each is the centre of attention some of the time.

Shyness

Most children go through a period of shyness at some stage. Build up confidence by emphasizing what they have to offer and what they're good at and encourage them to be helpful to other children who may feel the same. But don't go on about their shyness until they believe it's a cross they're destined to carry forever, and never mention it to other people when they are present.

Teach your child 'opening strategies': what to say to strangers or how to offer a toy to share. Don't take the easy way out and avoid group play. Yes, your child may have difficulty at first, but retreating only intensifies the problem.

Never underestimate your own role in your child's self-confidence. Each time you listen to what she has to say with interest, you are saying 'Your opinions matter. You are important.' I know how difficult it can be to concentrate when you have one eye on the cooker and the other on your watch, but laying the foundation of your child's future matters more in the long run than most day-to-day affairs.

Don't fall into the nagging habit. 'You're always dirtying your shoes' or 'Why do you make so much noise?' are off-the-cuff remarks with little venomous intent, but they can give unconfident children the impression that they're a drag on you. It is better to reward than punish, but the reward may be simply 'I knew you'd be able to manage that,' which implies your trust in their ability.

Another confidence-booster is to allow the child a degree of control over her own affairs. 'What do you want to wear today?'

or, 'Do you want to keep your toys here?' is enough. And if you can let her extend that choice to family affairs, all the better. 'I was thinking of putting that clock over there. What do you think?' is emphasizing the child's place in the family hierarchy as someone with the right to an opinion. Sometimes that opinion will prevail and the advice be followed. Sometimes it won't. And that 'win some, lose some' formula is another valuable lesson.

CRISES

A small child has no experience of survival, so a crisis can seem like the end of the world. Helping children through crisis and teaching them coping strategies is vital, and yet too often their emotional needs are neglected in favour of attending to their physical wants.

Keeping life normal

Children packed off to neighbours in the wake of a family death may be safe, warm and fed, but their overwhelming impression is of a world – their world – in disintegration. They are seldom 'better off out of it' unless there is the chance of real physical danger – and unless the place they are going to is familiar and as much like a second home as possible.

Try to keep their routine and their surroundings as normal as possible. And be sure to explain what is happening and why you may be sad or on edge. Again, just as with protecting them against the dangers of abduction or abuse, there is no need to go into great detail, but do be prepared to answer their questions.

Death

It is tempting to indoctrinate your children with your own religious beliefs, especially when someone dies. Saying, 'Grandma has gone to Heaven,' comforts you both if you have a religious faith. In this area, you should obey your instincts. If you choose, you can say 'I believe' or 'I don't know,' but in either case emphasize that what has happened is part of life.

Remind your children of happy times and how much they were loved by the one they have lost. 'Grandpa always liked you to be happy,' is both true and comforting, and allows a child not to feel guilty about having fun in the aftermath of death.

Above all, try to keep life as normal as possible. Of course, this does not mean that you should pretend that there has been no loss; it means that children need a sense of continuity. If you cry, don't apologize but let them see that tears eventually dry and nice things still happen. If you can, celebrate the person who has left the family scene.

In the wake of his father's death, I took my young son to a place we had loved to visit as a family. It was both painful and cathartic and allowed us to talk freely of the pain of the present, our hopes for the future, and how important a part Daddy would still play in our lives.

Divorce

When lives are disrupted by separation or divorce, make sure the child is prepared. All too often, children aren't told until mum's or dad's bags are packed and waiting in the hall.

Allow children time to adjust, but never suggest that the parting might never happen. Emphasize how much cooperation there will be and the advantages of having two residences. As man and woman, you may be separating. As parents, you never can.

Hospital

When illness strikes or children have to be admitted to hospital, it's important to stress that their place in the family will remain. Talk about plans for their bedroom when they return; show them a visiting roster and tell them exactly what family members will be doing while they are away.

With small children, a 'mystery' parcel to be opened at the end of visiting can be a useful antidote to tears on parting. Make sure the nursing staff know your child's likes and dislikes and the name by which he likes to be called. Be patient with moods or tantrums. Being in hospital can be a scary experience even for adults.

Redundancy

If the family is hit by job loss or business failure, don't try to keep it from children. They know when parents are tense and can usually conjure up the wildest reasons for that tension.

Emphasize that the loss of a job is not the end of the world, and let them know what is happening, step by step. Again, there is no need to tell them the wolf is at the door. They don't need lies, but they need only as much truth as they can manage.

Moving house

When moving house, understand your child's reluctance to lose those ties he has made with his neighbourhood. Promise to bring him back to visit friends or, if this is geographically impossible, arrange contact by phone or letter.

Saying 'You'll make new friends' is not enough. At this moment he doesn't want new friends; he wants to keep those he already has. In time, most of the ties will be relinquished, but for now he needs to believe they can be retained.

If possible, arrange visits to new schools well in advance and consult him on how the new house should be laid out. Taking photographs of friends and scenes left behind can help. In three or four months they'll be put to one side, but for now they are balm.

Loss of a pet

When a well-loved pet dies, stress how happy its life was and how it will never be forgotten by the family.

When a pet goes missing, the situation is more difficult. Show that you have done your best to find it and then point out that there is a good chance that someone, somewhere, will take it in and love it, too. While this may or may not be true, it does help a child to know that organizations exist that help lost and stray animals.

Loss of a toy

If a well-loved toy is lost, search diligently, but if it cannot be found, say that someone probably has found it, and will love it as we loved it. A child needs a resolution.

Trauma

After a trauma such as a severe accident or sexual abuse, it is vital not to treat your child as 'damaged goods'. I believe that sometimes more abuse occurs after the event than during it, as children are paraded as victims, forever despoiled.

Be prepared to talk about their trauma, but don't make it the axle around which the family revolves. The utter normalcy of family life can be the healing agent a victim badly needs.

Disability

Self-confidence is particularly important for children who have a disability or a chronic illness. If they know that their inability to perform certain functions is matched by a talent in other directions, it will do much to compensate.

Knowing their opinion matters gives them an equal status within the home. Make full use of the organizations that exist to help parents in this situation (pages 184–7).

useful information

Registering a birth

Every baby born in the United Kingdom must be registered by one of its parents with the registrar of births and deaths for the district in which the child is born. In England and Wales, registration must be made within forty days of birth; in Scotland, within twenty-one days.

Whoever delivered your baby will give you a birth-notification form to pass on to the registrar. If you're not married, your partner must also be there to put his name on the birth certificate. You need a name for the baby in order to register it, but you can change it later, should you wish, for a small fee.

Once the name of your child has been registered, you can start claiming child benefit. Get a claim form from your local Social Security Office.

If, for some reason, you should lose your child's birth certificate, you can get a replacement (for a small fee) either by going to the public search rooms of the General Register Office:

Family Records Centre
1 Middleton Street
London EC1R 1UW

or by applying by post to:

General Register Office
Smedley Hydro, Trafalgar Road
Merseyside PR8 2HH

You can also find out information about certificates by phone on 0870 243 77 88, or via email from certificate.services@ons.gov.uk.

Immunizations

The Department of Health recommends that all children should be immunized against the following diseases.

At two months:
Hib, an influenza virus which causes a range of illness including a type of meningitis

At two, three, and four months:
Diphtheria, whooping cough, tetanus and polio

At twelve to fifteen months:
Measles, mumps and rubella

At three to five years:
Diphtheria, tetanus and polio (booster)

At ten to fourteen years:
Rubella (girls only)

At ten to fourteen years:
TB

At sixteen:
Tetanus and diphtheria

At fifteen to nineteen years:
Polio

Parental responsibility and rights of access

In the UK, a natural father has no legal right to parental responsibility if he is not married to the mother and his name isn't on the birth certificate (this may change when the Adoption and Children Bill goes through Parliament).

A father can acquire parental responsibility if the mother agrees, or by obtaining a court order. If the absent father maintains the child, that does not mean he has parental responsibility unless he fulfils the criteria just described.

Once a father has acquired parental responsibility, he would automatically become the child's guardian in the event of the mother's death. Seeking legal advice about a parental responsibility order can save future arguments.

In matters of access, the Lord Chancellor's Department has produced a parenting plan that can help; Family Mediation can also play a useful role. If there has been physical or emotional abuse, get legal advice before a difficult situation develops. If you don't already know and trust a solicitor, talk to the local Citizens Advice Bureau.

If you are completely alone and have to relinquish custody of your child while you go into hospital or recover from illness, Social Services can help. Your child must be returned to you when you ask (unless there is a court order forbidding this), and you retain parental responsibility during the separation.

Before contacting Social Services, it is helpful to contact the Family Rights Group or your local Citizens Advice Bureau. In all matters involving single parents, the National Council for One-Parent Families can help (see page 187).

Helpful organizations and support groups

Association for Post-natal Illness
+44 (0) 207 386 0868

BLISS (Premature babies)
+44 (0) 870 7700 337

Breast Feeding Line (NCT)
+44 (0) 870 444 8708

British Allergy Foundation
+44 (0) 208 303 8583

Careline
+44 (0) 208 514 1177
For parents and children.

Child Benefit Centre
+44 (0) 8701 555 540

Child Support Agency
+44 (0) 8457 133 133

Childline
+44 (0) 800 11 11

Children's Legal Centre
+44 (0) 1206 87 38 20

Contact a Family
+44 (0) 808 808 3555

The Child Psychotherapy Trust
+44 (0) 207 284 1355

The Cot Death Society
+44 (0) 845 601 0234

Council for Disabled Children
+44 (0) 207 843 6061

CRY-SIS
+44 (0) 207 404 5011

Dyspraxia Foundation
+44 (0) 1462 454 986

Families Need Fathers
+44 (0) 207 613 5060

Family Contact Line
+44 (0) 161 941 4011
For parents with children from baby to school age.
Provides flexible services to relieve family stresses,
especially if feeling lonely or isolated.

Family Rights Group
+44 (0) 800 731 1696

Fathers Direct
+44 (0) 207 920 9491

Gingerbread Advice Line
+44 (0) 800 018 4318

Homestart
+44 (0) 800 068 6368
Help for families under stress.

Kidscape
+44 (0) 8451 205 204
Bullying helpline.

**Look (The National Federation of Families
with Visually Impaired Children)**
+44 (0) 121 428 5038

Maternity Alliance
+44 (0) 207 588 8583

The National Autistic Society
+44 (0) 870 600 8585

National Childbirth Trust (NCT)
+44 (0) 870 444 8707

National Child-minding Association
+44 (0) 208 464 6164

National Council for One-Parent families
+44 (0) 800 018 5026

National Family Mediation
+44 (0) 207 485 8809

NHS Direct
+44 (0) 845 46 47

National Society for the Prevention of Cruelty to Children (NSPCC)
+44 (0) 808 800 5000

ParenTalk
+44 (0) 700 2000 500

Parentline
+44 (0) 808 800 2222

Pre-school Learning Alliance
+44 (0) 207 833 0991

SANDS (Stillbirth and Neonatal Deaths)
+44 (0) 207 436 5881

Single Parent Action
+44 (0) 117 951 4231

Twinline
+44 (0) 1732 868 000
Helpline for parents of twins, triplets or more.

Twins & Multiple Birth Association
+44 (0) 870 770 3305

Young Minds
+44 (0) 800 018 2138
For children with emotional or behavioural problems.

INDEX

192 *how to be a good parent*